Welcome to Our Humble Commode!

PLEASE SIGN OUR GUEST BOOK.
IT'S SOMETHING TO DO,
WHILE YOU DO WHAT YOU DOO.

Welcome! PLEASE SEAT YOURSELF AND ENJOY YOUR VISIT!

NAME: _____ DATE: _____ TIME: _____ DURATION OF VISIT: _____
HRS   MIN   SEC

PURPOSE FOR VISIT: ☐ #1 ☐ #2 ☐ OTHER: _____ SUCCESS? ☐ YES ☐ NO

FAVORITE EUPHEMISM FOR PERFORMING #1:

FAVORITE RESTROOM GRAFFITI OR YOUR ORIGNAL DOODLE:

FAVORITE EUPHEMISM FOR PERFORMING #2:

WHILE YOU WERE HERE, DID YOU:
- ☐ TEXT SOMEONE
- ☐ MAKE A PHONE CALL
- ☐ EMAIL
- ☐ CHECK SOCIAL MEDIA
- ☐ TAKE A SELFIE
- ☐ LOOK IN THE MEDICINE CABINET
- ☐ CHECK YOUR TEETH
- ☐ CHECK OUT YOUR BUTT
- ☐ CHECK YOUR FLY
- ☐ READ
- ☐ FIX YOUR HAIR
- ☐ TAKE SOME EXTRA "ME TIME"
- ☐ TALK TO YOURSELF
- ☐ CONDUCT BUSINESS OTHER THAN YOUR "BUSINESS." CARE TO SHARE?
_____

FAVORITE NAME FOR THIS ROOM:
- ☐ BATHROOM
- ☐ TOILET
- ☐ POWDER ROOM
- ☐ LAVATORY
- ☐ SHITTER
- ☐ LOO
- ☐ LITTLE GIRLS ROOM
- ☐ LITTLE BOYS ROOM
- ☐ COMFORT STATION
- ☐ OTHER: _____
- ☐ JOHN
- ☐ CAN
- ☐ HEAD
- ☐ POTTY
- ☐ CRAPPER
- ☐ WC

_____

RATINGS: 1 2 3 4 5
CLEANLINESS   ☆ ☆ ☆ ☆ ☆
AMBIENCE   ☆ ☆ ☆ ☆ ☆
AMENITIES   ☆ ☆ ☆ ☆ ☆
SOUND PROOFING   ☆ ☆ ☆ ☆ ☆
QUALITY OF THE FLUSH   ☆ ☆ ☆ ☆ ☆
TOILET PAPER   ☆ ☆ ☆ ☆ ☆

OVERALL EXPERIENCE:
- ☐ BEST SEAT IN THE HOUSE   ★ ★ ★ ★ ★
- ☐ WOULD POOP HERE AGAIN   ★ ★ ★ ★
- ☐ SHIT GOT REAL   ★ ★ ★
- ☐ SAME SHIT DIFFERENT HOUSE   ★ ★
- ☐ THINGS JUST DIDN'T COME OUT RIGHT ★

THOUGHTS/MESSAGES: _____
_____
_____

Welcome! PLEASE SEAT YOURSELF AND ENJOY YOUR VISIT!

NAME: _____   DATE: _____   TIME: _____   DURATION OF VISIT: _____
                                                                    HRS   MIN   SEC

PURPOSE FOR VISIT: ▢ #1   ▢ #2   ▢ OTHER: _____   SUCCESS? ▢ YES ▢ NO

FAVORITE EUPHEMISM FOR PERFORMING #1:

FAVORITE RESTROOM GRAFFITI OR YOUR ORIGNAL DOODLE:

FAVORITE EUPHEMISM FOR PERFORMING #2:

WHILE YOU WERE HERE, DID YOU:
- ☐ TEXT SOMEONE
- ☐ MAKE A PHONE CALL
- ☐ EMAIL
- ☐ CHECK SOCIAL MEDIA
- ☐ TAKE A SELFIE
- ☐ LOOK IN THE MEDICINE CABINET
- ☐ CHECK YOUR TEETH
- ☐ CHECK OUT YOUR BUTT
- ☐ CHECK YOUR FLY
- ☐ READ
- ☐ FIX YOUR HAIR
- ☐ TAKE SOME EXTRA "ME TIME"
- ☐ TALK TO YOURSELF
- ☐ CONDUCT BUSINESS OTHER THAN YOUR "BUSINESS." CARE TO SHARE?
  _____

FAVORITE NAME FOR THIS ROOM:
- ☐ BATHROOM
- ☐ TOILET
- ☐ POWDER ROOM
- ☐ LAVATORY
- ☐ SHITTER
- ☐ LOO
- ☐ LITTLE GIRLS ROOM
- ☐ LITTLE BOYS ROOM
- ☐ COMFORT STATION
- ☐ JOHN
- ☐ CAN
- ☐ HEAD
- ☐ POTTY
- ☐ CRAPPER
- ☐ WC
- ☐ OTHER: _____

_____

RATINGS:

	1	2	3	4	5
CLEANLINESS	☆	☆	☆	☆	☆
AMBIENCE	☆	☆	☆	☆	☆
AMENITIES	☆	☆	☆	☆	☆
SOUND PROOFING	☆	☆	☆	☆	☆
QUALITY OF THE FLUSH	☆	☆	☆	☆	☆
TOILET PAPER	☆	☆	☆	☆	☆

OVERALL EXPERIENCE:
- ☐ BEST SEAT IN THE HOUSE ★ ★ ★ ★ ★
- ☐ WOULD POOP HERE AGAIN ★ ★ ★ ★
- ☐ SHIT GOT REAL ★ ★ ★
- ☐ SAME SHIT DIFFERENT HOUSE ★ ★
- ☐ THINGS JUST DIDN'T COME OUT RIGHT ★

THOUGHTS/MESSAGES: _____
_____
_____

Welcome! PLEASE SEAT YOURSELF AND ENJOY YOUR VISIT!

NAME: _____ DATE: _____ TIME: _____ DURATION OF VISIT: _____
HRS   MIN   SEC

PURPOSE FOR VISIT: ▢ #1 ▢ #2 ▢ OTHER: _____ SUCCESS? ▢ YES ▢ NO

FAVORITE EUPHEMISM FOR PERFORMING #1:

FAVORITE RESTROOM GRAFFITI OR YOUR ORIGNAL DOODLE:

FAVORITE EUPHEMISM FOR PERFORMING #2:

WHILE YOU WERE HERE, DID YOU:
- ▢ TEXT SOMEONE
- ▢ MAKE A PHONE CALL
- ▢ EMAIL
- ▢ CHECK SOCIAL MEDIA
- ▢ TAKE A SELFIE
- ▢ LOOK IN THE MEDICINE CABINET
- ▢ CHECK YOUR TEETH
- ▢ CHECK OUT YOUR BUTT
- ▢ CHECK YOUR FLY
- ▢ READ
- ▢ FIX YOUR HAIR
- ▢ TAKE SOME EXTRA "ME TIME"
- ▢ TALK TO YOURSELF
- ▢ CONDUCT BUSINESS OTHER THAN YOUR "BUSINESS," CARE TO SHARE?
_____

FAVORITE NAME FOR THIS ROOM:
- ▢ BATHROOM
- ▢ TOILET
- ▢ POWDER ROOM
- ▢ LAVATORY
- ▢ SHITTER
- ▢ LOO
- ▢ LITTLE GIRLS ROOM
- ▢ LITTLE BOYS ROOM
- ▢ COMFORT STATION
- ▢ OTHER: _____
- ▢ JOHN
- ▢ CAN
- ▢ HEAD
- ▢ POTTY
- ▢ CRAPPER
- ▢ WC

RATINGS:
	1	2	3	4	5
CLEANLINESS	☆	☆	☆	☆	☆
AMBIENCE	☆	☆	☆	☆	☆
AMENITIES	☆	☆	☆	☆	☆
SOUND PROOFING	☆	☆	☆	☆	☆
QUALITY OF THE FLUSH	☆	☆	☆	☆	☆
TOILET PAPER	☆	☆	☆	☆	☆

OVERALL EXPERIENCE:
- ▢ BEST SEAT IN THE HOUSE ★ ★ ★ ★ ★
- ▢ WOULD POOP HERE AGAIN ★ ★ ★ ★
- ▢ SHIT GOT REAL ★ ★ ★
- ▢ SAME SHIT DIFFERENT HOUSE ★ ★
- ▢ THINGS JUST DIDN'T COME OUT RIGHT ★

THOUGHTS/MESSAGES: _____
_____

Welcome! PLEASE SEAT YOURSELF AND ENJOY YOUR VISIT!

NAME: _____ DATE: _____ TIME: _____ DURATION OF VISIT: _____
HRS   MIN   SEC

PURPOSE FOR VISIT: 🧻 #1   🧻 #2   🧻 OTHER: _____   SUCCESS? 🧻 YES   🧻 NO

FAVORITE EUPHEMISM FOR PERFORMING #1:

FAVORITE EUPHEMISM FOR PERFORMING #2:

FAVORITE RESTROOM GRAFFITI OR YOUR ORIGNAL DOODLE:

WHILE YOU WERE HERE, DID YOU:
- ☐ TEXT SOMEONE
- ☐ MAKE A PHONE CALL
- ☐ EMAIL
- ☐ CHECK SOCIAL MEDIA
- ☐ TAKE A SELFIE
- ☐ LOOK IN THE MEDICINE CABINET
- ☐ CHECK YOUR TEETH
- ☐ CHECK OUT YOUR BUTT
- ☐ CHECK YOUR FLY
- ☐ READ
- ☐ FIX YOUR HAIR
- ☐ TAKE SOME EXTRA "ME TIME"
- ☐ TALK TO YOURSELF
- ☐ CONDUCT BUSINESS OTHER THAN YOUR "BUSINESS." CARE TO SHARE?

FAVORITE NAME FOR THIS ROOM:
- ☐ BATHROOM
- ☐ TOILET
- ☐ POWDER ROOM
- ☐ LAVATORY
- ☐ SHITTER
- ☐ LOO
- ☐ LITTLE GIRLS ROOM
- ☐ LITTLE BOYS ROOM
- ☐ COMFORT STATION
- ☐ OTHER: _____
- ☐ JOHN
- ☐ CAN
- ☐ HEAD
- ☐ POTTY
- ☐ CRAPPER
- ☐ WC

RATINGS:

	1	2	3	4	5
CLEANLINESS	☆	☆	☆	☆	☆
AMBIENCE	☆	☆	☆	☆	☆
AMENITIES	☆	☆	☆	☆	☆
SOUND PROOFING	☆	☆	☆	☆	☆
QUALITY OF THE FLUSH	☆	☆	☆	☆	☆
TOILET PAPER	☆	☆	☆	☆	☆

OVERALL EXPERIENCE:
- ☐ BEST SEAT IN THE HOUSE ★ ★ ★ ★ ★
- ☐ WOULD POOP HERE AGAIN ★ ★ ★ ★
- ☐ SHIT GOT REAL ★ ★ ★
- ☐ SAME SHIT DIFFERENT HOUSE ★ ★
- ☐ THINGS JUST DIDN'T COME OUT RIGHT ★

THOUGHTS/MESSAGES: _____

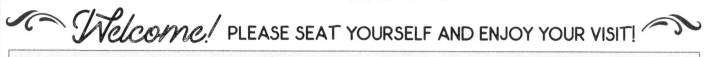

Welcome! PLEASE SEAT YOURSELF AND ENJOY YOUR VISIT!

NAME: _____ DATE: _____ TIME: _____ DURATION OF VISIT: _____
HRS   MIN   SEC

PURPOSE FOR VISIT: 🧻 #1 🧻 #2 🧻 OTHER: _____ SUCCESS? 🧻 YES 🧻 NO

FAVORITE EUPHEMISM FOR PERFORMING #1: | FAVORITE RESTROOM GRAFFITI OR YOUR ORIGNAL DOODLE:

FAVORITE EUPHEMISM FOR PERFORMING #2:

WHILE YOU WERE HERE, DID YOU:
- ☐ TEXT SOMEONE
- ☐ MAKE A PHONE CALL
- ☐ EMAIL
- ☐ CHECK SOCIAL MEDIA
- ☐ TAKE A SELFIE
- ☐ LOOK IN THE MEDICINE CABINET
- ☐ CHECK YOUR TEETH
- ☐ CHECK OUT YOUR BUTT
- ☐ CHECK YOUR FLY
- ☐ READ
- ☐ FIX YOUR HAIR
- ☐ TAKE SOME EXTRA "ME TIME"
- ☐ TALK TO YOURSELF
- ☐ CONDUCT BUSINESS OTHER THAN YOUR "BUSINESS." CARE TO SHARE?
  _____

FAVORITE NAME FOR THIS ROOM:
- ☐ BATHROOM
- ☐ TOILET
- ☐ POWDER ROOM
- ☐ LAVATORY
- ☐ SHITTER
- ☐ LOO
- ☐ LITTLE GIRLS ROOM
- ☐ LITTLE BOYS ROOM
- ☐ COMFORT STATION
- ☐ OTHER: _____
- ☐ JOHN
- ☐ CAN
- ☐ HEAD
- ☐ POTTY
- ☐ CRAPPER
- ☐ WC

_____
_____

RATINGS:
	1	2	3	4	5
CLEANLINESS	☆	☆	☆	☆	☆
AMBIENCE	☆	☆	☆	☆	☆
AMENITIES	☆	☆	☆	☆	☆
SOUND PROOFING	☆	☆	☆	☆	☆
QUALITY OF THE FLUSH	☆	☆	☆	☆	☆
TOILET PAPER	☆	☆	☆	☆	☆

OVERALL EXPERIENCE:
- ☐ BEST SEAT IN THE HOUSE ★★★★★
- ☐ WOULD POOP HERE AGAIN ★★★★
- ☐ SHIT GOT REAL ★★★
- ☐ SAME SHIT DIFFERENT HOUSE ★★
- ☐ THINGS JUST DIDN'T COME OUT RIGHT ★

THOUGHTS/MESSAGES: _____
_____
_____

Welcome! PLEASE SEAT YOURSELF AND ENJOY YOUR VISIT!

NAME: _____ DATE:_____ TIME: _____ DURATION OF VISIT: _____
HRS   MIN   SEC

PURPOSE FOR VISIT: [ ] #1   [ ] #2   [ ] OTHER: _____   SUCCESS? [ ] YES [ ] NO

FAVORITE EUPHEMISM FOR PERFORMING #1:

FAVORITE EUPHEMISM FOR PERFORMING #2:

FAVORITE RESTROOM GRAFFITI OR YOUR ORIGNAL DOODLE:

WHILE YOU WERE HERE, DID YOU:
- ☐ TEXT SOMEONE
- ☐ MAKE A PHONE CALL
- ☐ EMAIL
- ☐ CHECK SOCIAL MEDIA
- ☐ TAKE A SELFIE
- ☐ LOOK IN THE MEDICINE CABINET
- ☐ CHECK YOUR TEETH
- ☐ CHECK OUT YOUR BUTT
- ☐ CHECK YOUR FLY
- ☐ READ
- ☐ FIX YOUR HAIR
- ☐ TAKE SOME EXTRA "ME TIME"
- ☐ TALK TO YOURSELF
- ☐ CONDUCT BUSINESS OTHER THAN YOUR "BUSINESS." CARE TO SHARE?

FAVORITE NAME FOR THIS ROOM:
- ☐ BATHROOM
- ☐ TOILET
- ☐ POWDER ROOM
- ☐ LAVATORY
- ☐ SHITTER
- ☐ LOO
- ☐ LITTLE GIRLS ROOM
- ☐ LITTLE BOYS ROOM
- ☐ COMFORT STATION
- ☐ OTHER: _____
- ☐ JOHN
- ☐ CAN
- ☐ HEAD
- ☐ POTTY
- ☐ CRAPPER
- ☐ WC

RATINGS:

	1	2	3	4	5
CLEANLINESS	☆	☆	☆	☆	☆
AMBIENCE	☆	☆	☆	☆	☆
AMENITIES	☆	☆	☆	☆	☆
SOUND PROOFING	☆	☆	☆	☆	☆
QUALITY OF THE FLUSH	☆	☆	☆	☆	☆
TOILET PAPER	☆	☆	☆	☆	☆

OVERALL EXPERIENCE:
- ☐ BEST SEAT IN THE HOUSE ★ ★ ★ ★ ★
- ☐ WOULD POOP HERE AGAIN ★ ★ ★ ★
- ☐ SHIT GOT REAL ★ ★ ★
- ☐ SAME SHIT DIFFERENT HOUSE ★ ★
- ☐ THINGS JUST DIDN'T COME OUT RIGHT ★

THOUGHTS/MESSAGES: _____
_____
_____

Welcome! PLEASE SEAT YOURSELF AND ENJOY YOUR VISIT!

NAME: _____ DATE: _____ TIME: _____ DURATION OF VISIT: _____

HRS   MIN   SEC

PURPOSE FOR VISIT: 🧻 #1 🧻 #2 🧻 OTHER: _____ SUCCESS? 🧻 YES 🧻 NO

FAVORITE EUPHEMISM FOR PERFORMING #1:

FAVORITE EUPHEMISM FOR PERFORMING #2:

FAVORITE RESTROOM GRAFFITI OR YOUR ORIGNAL DOODLE:

WHILE YOU WERE HERE, DID YOU:
- ☐ TEXT SOMEONE
- ☐ MAKE A PHONE CALL
- ☐ EMAIL
- ☐ CHECK SOCIAL MEDIA
- ☐ TAKE A SELFIE
- ☐ LOOK IN THE MEDICINE CABINET
- ☐ CHECK YOUR TEETH
- ☐ CHECK OUT YOUR BUTT
- ☐ CHECK YOUR FLY
- ☐ READ
- ☐ FIX YOUR HAIR
- ☐ TAKE SOME EXTRA "ME TIME"
- ☐ TALK TO YOURSELF
- ☐ CONDUCT BUSINESS OTHER THAN YOUR "BUSINESS." CARE TO SHARE?

FAVORITE NAME FOR THIS ROOM:
- ☐ BATHROOM
- ☐ TOILET
- ☐ POWDER ROOM
- ☐ LAVATORY
- ☐ SHITTER
- ☐ LOO
- ☐ LITTLE GIRLS ROOM
- ☐ LITTLE BOYS ROOM
- ☐ COMFORT STATION
- ☐ OTHER: _____
- ☐ JOHN
- ☐ CAN
- ☐ HEAD
- ☐ POTTY
- ☐ CRAPPER
- ☐ WC

RATINGS: 1 2 3 4 5
CLEANLINESS   ☆ ☆ ☆ ☆ ☆
AMBIENCE   ☆ ☆ ☆ ☆ ☆
AMENITIES   ☆ ☆ ☆ ☆ ☆
SOUND PROOFING   ☆ ☆ ☆ ☆ ☆
QUALITY OF THE FLUSH   ☆ ☆ ☆ ☆ ☆
TOILET PAPER   ☆ ☆ ☆ ☆ ☆

OVERALL EXPERIENCE:
- ☐ BEST SEAT IN THE HOUSE ★ ★ ★ ★ ★
- ☐ WOULD POOP HERE AGAIN   ★ ★ ★ ★
- ☐ SHIT GOT REAL   ★ ★ ★
- ☐ SAME SHIT DIFFERENT HOUSE   ★ ★
- ☐ THINGS JUST DIDN'T COME OUT RIGHT ★

THOUGHTS/MESSAGES: _____
_____
_____

Welcome! PLEASE SEAT YOURSELF AND ENJOY YOUR VISIT!

NAME: _____ DATE: _____ TIME: _____ DURATION OF VISIT: _____
HRS   MIN   SEC

PURPOSE FOR VISIT: 🧻 #1   🧻 #2   🧻 OTHER: _____   SUCCESS? 🧻 YES 🧻 NO

FAVORITE EUPHEMISM FOR PERFORMING #1:

FAVORITE RESTROOM GRAFFITI OR YOUR ORIGNAL DOODLE:

FAVORITE EUPHEMISM FOR PERFORMING #2:

WHILE YOU WERE HERE, DID YOU:
- ☐ TEXT SOMEONE
- ☐ MAKE A PHONE CALL
- ☐ EMAIL
- ☐ CHECK SOCIAL MEDIA
- ☐ TAKE A SELFIE
- ☐ LOOK IN THE MEDICINE CABINET
- ☐ CHECK YOUR TEETH
- ☐ CHECK OUT YOUR BUTT
- ☐ CHECK YOUR FLY
- ☐ READ
- ☐ FIX YOUR HAIR
- ☐ TAKE SOME EXTRA "ME TIME"
- ☐ TALK TO YOURSELF
- ☐ CONDUCT BUSINESS OTHER THAN YOUR "BUSINESS." CARE TO SHARE?

FAVORITE NAME FOR THIS ROOM:
- ☐ BATHROOM
- ☐ TOILET
- ☐ POWDER ROOM
- ☐ LAVATORY
- ☐ SHITTER
- ☐ LOO
- ☐ LITTLE GIRLS ROOM
- ☐ LITTLE BOYS ROOM
- ☐ COMFORT STATION
- ☐ OTHER: _____
- ☐ JOHN
- ☐ CAN
- ☐ HEAD
- ☐ POTTY
- ☐ CRAPPER
- ☐ WC

_____

RATINGS: 1 2 3 4 5

	1	2	3	4	5
CLEANLINESS	☆	☆	☆	☆	☆
AMBIENCE	☆	☆	☆	☆	☆
AMENITIES	☆	☆	☆	☆	☆
SOUND PROOFING	☆	☆	☆	☆	☆
QUALITY OF THE FLUSH	☆	☆	☆	☆	☆
TOILET PAPER	☆	☆	☆	☆	☆

OVERALL EXPERIENCE:
- ☐ BEST SEAT IN THE HOUSE ★ ★ ★ ★ ★
- ☐ WOULD POOP HERE AGAIN ★ ★ ★ ★
- ☐ SHIT GOT REAL ★ ★ ★
- ☐ SAME SHIT DIFFERENT HOUSE ★ ★
- ☐ THINGS JUST DIDN'T COME OUT RIGHT ★

THOUGHTS/MESSAGES: _____
_____
_____

Welcome! PLEASE SEAT YOURSELF AND ENJOY YOUR VISIT!

NAME: _____ DATE: _____ TIME: _____ DURATION OF VISIT: _____
HRS   MIN   SEC

PURPOSE FOR VISIT: ▢ #1 ▢ #2 ▢ OTHER: _____ SUCCESS? ▢ YES ▢ NO

FAVORITE EUPHEMISM FOR PERFORMING #1:

FAVORITE RESTROOM GRAFFITI OR YOUR ORIGNAL DOODLE:

FAVORITE EUPHEMISM FOR PERFORMING #2:

WHILE YOU WERE HERE, DID YOU:
- ☐ TEXT SOMEONE
- ☐ MAKE A PHONE CALL
- ☐ EMAIL
- ☐ CHECK SOCIAL MEDIA
- ☐ TAKE A SELFIE
- ☐ LOOK IN THE MEDICINE CABINET
- ☐ CHECK YOUR TEETH
- ☐ CHECK OUT YOUR BUTT
- ☐ CHECK YOUR FLY
- ☐ READ
- ☐ FIX YOUR HAIR
- ☐ TAKE SOME EXTRA "ME TIME"
- ☐ TALK TO YOURSELF
- ☐ CONDUCT BUSINESS OTHER THAN YOUR "BUSINESS." CARE TO SHARE?

FAVORITE NAME FOR THIS ROOM:
- ☐ BATHROOM
- ☐ TOILET
- ☐ POWDER ROOM
- ☐ LAVATORY
- ☐ SHITTER
- ☐ LOO
- ☐ LITTLE GIRLS ROOM
- ☐ LITTLE BOYS ROOM
- ☐ COMFORT STATION
- ☐ OTHER: _____
- ☐ JOHN
- ☐ CAN
- ☐ HEAD
- ☐ POTTY
- ☐ CRAPPER
- ☐ WC

RATINGS:
	1	2	3	4	5
CLEANLINESS	☆	☆	☆	☆	☆
AMBIENCE	☆	☆	☆	☆	☆
AMENITIES	☆	☆	☆	☆	☆
SOUND PROOFING	☆	☆	☆	☆	☆
QUALITY OF THE FLUSH	☆	☆	☆	☆	☆
TOILET PAPER	☆	☆	☆	☆	☆

OVERALL EXPERIENCE:
- ☐ BEST SEAT IN THE HOUSE ★ ★ ★ ★ ★
- ☐ WOULD POOP HERE AGAIN ★ ★ ★ ★
- ☐ SHIT GOT REAL ★ ★ ★
- ☐ SAME SHIT DIFFERENT HOUSE ★ ★
- ☐ THINGS JUST DIDN'T COME OUT RIGHT ★

THOUGHTS/MESSAGES: _____
_____
_____

Welcome! PLEASE SEAT YOURSELF AND ENJOY YOUR VISIT!

NAME: _____ DATE: _____ TIME: _____ DURATION OF VISIT: _____
HRS   MIN   SEC

PURPOSE FOR VISIT: ☐ #1 ☐ #2 ☐ OTHER: _____ SUCCESS? ☐ YES ☐ NO

FAVORITE EUPHEMISM FOR PERFORMING #1:   FAVORITE RESTROOM GRAFFITI OR YOUR ORIGNAL DOODLE:

FAVORITE EUPHEMISM FOR PERFORMING #2:

WHILE YOU WERE HERE, DID YOU:
☐ TEXT SOMEONE
☐ MAKE A PHONE CALL
☐ EMAIL
☐ CHECK SOCIAL MEDIA
☐ TAKE A SELFIE
☐ LOOK IN THE MEDICINE CABINET
☐ CHECK YOUR TEETH
☐ CHECK OUT YOUR BUTT
☐ CHECK YOUR FLY
☐ READ
☐ FIX YOUR HAIR
☐ TAKE SOME EXTRA "ME TIME"
☐ TALK TO YOURSELF
☐ CONDUCT BUSINESS OTHER THAN YOUR "BUSINESS." CARE TO SHARE?
_____

FAVORITE NAME FOR THIS ROOM:
☐ BATHROOM   ☐ JOHN
☐ TOILET   ☐ CAN
☐ POWDER ROOM   ☐ HEAD
☐ LAVATORY   ☐ POTTY
☐ SHITTER   ☐ CRAPPER
☐ LOO   ☐ WC
☐ LITTLE GIRLS ROOM
☐ LITTLE BOYS ROOM
☐ COMFORT STATION
☐ OTHER: _____
_____

RATINGS: 1 2 3 4 5
CLEANLINESS   ☆ ☆ ☆ ☆ ☆
AMBIENCE   ☆ ☆ ☆ ☆ ☆
AMENITIES   ☆ ☆ ☆ ☆ ☆
SOUND PROOFING   ☆ ☆ ☆ ☆ ☆
QUALITY OF THE FLUSH ☆ ☆ ☆ ☆ ☆
TOILET PAPER   ☆ ☆ ☆ ☆ ☆

OVERALL EXPERIENCE:
☐ BEST SEAT IN THE HOUSE   ★ ★ ★ ★ ★
☐ WOULD POOP HERE AGAIN   ★ ★ ★ ★
☐ SHIT GOT REAL   ★ ★ ★
☐ SAME SHIT DIFFERENT HOUSE   ★ ★
☐ THINGS JUST DIDN'T COME OUT RIGHT ★

THOUGHTS/MESSAGES: _____
_____
_____

Welcome! PLEASE SEAT YOURSELF AND ENJOY YOUR VISIT!

NAME: _____ DATE: _____ TIME: _____ DURATION OF VISIT: _____
HRS   MIN   SEC

PURPOSE FOR VISIT: ☐ #1 ☐ #2 ☐ OTHER: _____ SUCCESS? ☐ YES ☐ NO

FAVORITE EUPHEMISM FOR PERFORMING #1:

FAVORITE RESTROOM GRAFFITI OR YOUR ORIGNAL DOODLE:

FAVORITE EUPHEMISM FOR PERFORMING #2:

WHILE YOU WERE HERE, DID YOU:
☐ TEXT SOMEONE
☐ MAKE A PHONE CALL
☐ EMAIL
☐ CHECK SOCIAL MEDIA
☐ TAKE A SELFIE
☐ LOOK IN THE MEDICINE CABINET
☐ CHECK YOUR TEETH
☐ CHECK OUT YOUR BUTT
☐ CHECK YOUR FLY
☐ READ
☐ FIX YOUR HAIR
☐ TAKE SOME EXTRA "ME TIME"
☐ TALK TO YOURSELF
☐ CONDUCT BUSINESS OTHER THAN YOUR "BUSINESS." CARE TO SHARE?
_____

FAVORITE NAME FOR THIS ROOM:
☐ BATHROOM   ☐ JOHN
☐ TOILET   ☐ CAN
☐ POWDER ROOM   ☐ HEAD
☐ LAVATORY   ☐ POTTY
☐ SHITTER   ☐ CRAPPER
☐ LOO   ☐ WC
☐ LITTLE GIRLS ROOM
☐ LITTLE BOYS ROOM
☐ COMFORT STATION
☐ OTHER: _____

_____

RATINGS: 1 2 3 4 5
CLEANLINESS   ☆ ☆ ☆ ☆ ☆
AMBIENCE   ☆ ☆ ☆ ☆ ☆
AMENITIES   ☆ ☆ ☆ ☆ ☆
SOUND PROOFING   ☆ ☆ ☆ ☆ ☆
QUALITY OF THE FLUSH   ☆ ☆ ☆ ☆ ☆
TOILET PAPER   ☆ ☆ ☆ ☆ ☆

OVERALL EXPERIENCE:
☐ BEST SEAT IN THE HOUSE   ★ ★ ★ ★ ★
☐ WOULD POOP HERE AGAIN   ★ ★ ★ ★
☐ SHIT GOT REAL   ★ ★ ★
☐ SAME SHIT DIFFERENT HOUSE   ★ ★
☐ THINGS JUST DIDN'T COME OUT RIGHT   ★

THOUGHTS/MESSAGES: _____
_____
_____

Welcome! PLEASE SEAT YOURSELF AND ENJOY YOUR VISIT!

NAME: _____ DATE: _____ TIME: _____ DURATION OF VISIT: _____
                                                                                    HRS   MIN   SEC

PURPOSE FOR VISIT: 🧻 #1 🧻 #2 🧻 OTHER: _____ SUCCESS? 🧻 YES 🧻 NO

FAVORITE EUPHEMISM FOR PERFORMING #1: | FAVORITE RESTROOM GRAFFITI OR YOUR ORIGNAL DOODLE:

FAVORITE EUPHEMISM FOR PERFORMING #2:

WHILE YOU WERE HERE, DID YOU:
☐ TEXT SOMEONE
☐ MAKE A PHONE CALL
☐ EMAIL
☐ CHECK SOCIAL MEDIA
☐ TAKE A SELFIE
☐ LOOK IN THE MEDICINE CABINET
☐ CHECK YOUR TEETH
☐ CHECK OUT YOUR BUTT
☐ CHECK YOUR FLY
☐ READ
☐ FIX YOUR HAIR
☐ TAKE SOME EXTRA "ME TIME"
☐ TALK TO YOURSELF
☐ CONDUCT BUSINESS OTHER THAN YOUR "BUSINESS." CARE TO SHARE?

FAVORITE NAME FOR THIS ROOM:
☐ BATHROOM   ☐ JOHN
☐ TOILET   ☐ CAN
☐ POWDER ROOM   ☐ HEAD
☐ LAVATORY   ☐ POTTY
☐ SHITTER   ☐ CRAPPER
☐ LOO   ☐ WC
☐ LITTLE GIRLS ROOM
☐ LITTLE BOYS ROOM
☐ COMFORT STATION
☐ OTHER: _____
_____

THOUGHTS/MESSAGES: _____
_____
_____

RATINGS: 1 2 3 4 5
CLEANLINESS   ☆ ☆ ☆ ☆ ☆
AMBIENCE   ☆ ☆ ☆ ☆ ☆
AMENITIES   ☆ ☆ ☆ ☆ ☆
SOUND PROOFING   ☆ ☆ ☆ ☆ ☆
QUALITY OF THE FLUSH   ☆ ☆ ☆ ☆ ☆
TOILET PAPER   ☆ ☆ ☆ ☆ ☆

OVERALL EXPERIENCE:
☐ BEST SEAT IN THE HOUSE   ★ ★ ★ ★ ★
☐ WOULD POOP HERE AGAIN   ★ ★ ★ ★
☐ SHIT GOT REAL   ★ ★ ★
☐ SAME SHIT DIFFERENT HOUSE   ★ ★
☐ THINGS JUST DIDN'T COME OUT RIGHT ★

Welcome! PLEASE SEAT YOURSELF AND ENJOY YOUR VISIT!

NAME: _____ DATE: _____ TIME: _____ DURATION OF VISIT: _____
                                                                                          HRS   MIN   SEC

PURPOSE FOR VISIT: ☐ #1 ☐ #2 ☐ OTHER: _____ SUCCESS? ☐ YES ☐ NO

FAVORITE EUPHEMISM FOR PERFORMING #1:

FAVORITE RESTROOM GRAFFITI OR YOUR ORIGNAL DOODLE:

FAVORITE EUPHEMISM FOR PERFORMING #2:

WHILE YOU WERE HERE, DID YOU:
- ☐ TEXT SOMEONE
- ☐ MAKE A PHONE CALL
- ☐ EMAIL
- ☐ CHECK SOCIAL MEDIA
- ☐ TAKE A SELFIE
- ☐ LOOK IN THE MEDICINE CABINET
- ☐ CHECK YOUR TEETH
- ☐ CHECK OUT YOUR BUTT
- ☐ CHECK YOUR FLY
- ☐ READ
- ☐ FIX YOUR HAIR
- ☐ TAKE SOME EXTRA "ME TIME"
- ☐ TALK TO YOURSELF
- ☐ CONDUCT BUSINESS OTHER THAN YOUR "BUSINESS." CARE TO SHARE?

FAVORITE NAME FOR THIS ROOM:
- ☐ BATHROOM
- ☐ TOILET
- ☐ POWDER ROOM
- ☐ LAVATORY
- ☐ SHITTER
- ☐ LOO
- ☐ LITTLE GIRLS ROOM
- ☐ LITTLE BOYS ROOM
- ☐ COMFORT STATION
- ☐ OTHER: _____
- ☐ JOHN
- ☐ CAN
- ☐ HEAD
- ☐ POTTY
- ☐ CRAPPER
- ☐ WC

RATINGS:
	1 2 3 4 5
CLEANLINESS	☆ ☆ ☆ ☆ ☆
AMBIENCE	☆ ☆ ☆ ☆ ☆
AMENITIES	☆ ☆ ☆ ☆ ☆
SOUND PROOFING	☆ ☆ ☆ ☆ ☆
QUALITY OF THE FLUSH	☆ ☆ ☆ ☆ ☆
TOILET PAPER	☆ ☆ ☆ ☆ ☆

OVERALL EXPERIENCE:
- ☐ BEST SEAT IN THE HOUSE ★ ★ ★ ★ ★
- ☐ WOULD POOP HERE AGAIN ★ ★ ★ ★
- ☐ SHIT GOT REAL ★ ★ ★
- ☐ SAME SHIT DIFFERENT HOUSE ★ ★
- ☐ THINGS JUST DIDN'T COME OUT RIGHT ★

THOUGHTS/MESSAGES: _____
_____
_____

Welcome! PLEASE SEAT YOURSELF AND ENJOY YOUR VISIT!

NAME: _____ DATE: _____ TIME: _____ DURATION OF VISIT: _____
                                                                              HRS   MIN   SEC

PURPOSE FOR VISIT: 🧻 #1   🧻 #2   🧻 OTHER: _____ SUCCESS? 🧻 YES   🧻 NO

FAVORITE EUPHEMISM FOR PERFORMING #1: | FAVORITE RESTROOM GRAFFITI OR YOUR ORIGNAL DOODLE:

FAVORITE EUPHEMISM FOR PERFORMING #2:

WHILE YOU WERE HERE, DID YOU:
- ☐ TEXT SOMEONE
- ☐ MAKE A PHONE CALL
- ☐ EMAIL
- ☐ CHECK SOCIAL MEDIA
- ☐ TAKE A SELFIE
- ☐ LOOK IN THE MEDICINE CABINET
- ☐ CHECK YOUR TEETH
- ☐ CHECK OUT YOUR BUTT
- ☐ CHECK YOUR FLY
- ☐ READ
- ☐ FIX YOUR HAIR
- ☐ TAKE SOME EXTRA "ME TIME"
- ☐ TALK TO YOURSELF
- ☐ CONDUCT BUSINESS OTHER THAN YOUR "BUSINESS." CARE TO SHARE? _____

FAVORITE NAME FOR THIS ROOM:
- ☐ BATHROOM
- ☐ TOILET
- ☐ POWDER ROOM
- ☐ LAVATORY
- ☐ SHITTER
- ☐ LOO
- ☐ LITTLE GIRLS ROOM
- ☐ LITTLE BOYS ROOM
- ☐ COMFORT STATION
- ☐ OTHER: _____
- ☐ JOHN
- ☐ CAN
- ☐ HEAD
- ☐ POTTY
- ☐ CRAPPER
- ☐ WC

RATINGS:

	1	2	3	4	5
CLEANLINESS	☆	☆	☆	☆	☆
AMBIENCE	☆	☆	☆	☆	☆
AMENITIES	☆	☆	☆	☆	☆
SOUND PROOFING	☆	☆	☆	☆	☆
QUALITY OF THE FLUSH	☆	☆	☆	☆	☆
TOILET PAPER	☆	☆	☆	☆	☆

OVERALL EXPERIENCE:
- ☐ BEST SEAT IN THE HOUSE ★★★★★
- ☐ WOULD POOP HERE AGAIN ★★★★
- ☐ SHIT GOT REAL ★★★
- ☐ SAME SHIT DIFFERENT HOUSE ★★
- ☐ THINGS JUST DIDN'T COME OUT RIGHT ★

THOUGHTS/MESSAGES: _____
_____
_____

Welcome! PLEASE SEAT YOURSELF AND ENJOY YOUR VISIT!

NAME: _____ DATE: _____ TIME: _____ DURATION OF VISIT: _____

HRS   MIN   SEC

PURPOSE FOR VISIT: ▢ #1   ▢ #2   ▢ OTHER: _____   SUCCESS? ▢ YES ▢ NO

FAVORITE EUPHEMISM FOR PERFORMING #1:

FAVORITE RESTROOM GRAFFITI OR YOUR ORIGNAL DOODLE:

FAVORITE EUPHEMISM FOR PERFORMING #2:

WHILE YOU WERE HERE, DID YOU:

☐ TEXT SOMEONE
☐ MAKE A PHONE CALL
☐ EMAIL
☐ CHECK SOCIAL MEDIA
☐ TAKE A SELFIE
☐ LOOK IN THE MEDICINE CABINET
☐ CHECK YOUR TEETH
☐ CHECK OUT YOUR BUTT
☐ CHECK YOUR FLY
☐ READ
☐ FIX YOUR HAIR
☐ TAKE SOME EXTRA "ME TIME"
☐ TALK TO YOURSELF
☐ CONDUCT BUSINESS OTHER THAN YOUR "BUSINESS." CARE TO SHARE?
_____

FAVORITE NAME FOR THIS ROOM:

☐ BATHROOM   ☐ JOHN
☐ TOILET   ☐ CAN
☐ POWDER ROOM   ☐ HEAD
☐ LAVATORY   ☐ POTTY
☐ SHITTER   ☐ CRAPPER
☐ LOO   ☐ WC
☐ LITTLE GIRLS ROOM
☐ LITTLE BOYS ROOM
☐ COMFORT STATION
☐ OTHER: _____
_____

RATINGS:

	1	2	3	4	5
CLEANLINESS	☆	☆	☆	☆	☆
AMBIENCE	☆	☆	☆	☆	☆
AMENITIES	☆	☆	☆	☆	☆
SOUND PROOFING	☆	☆	☆	☆	☆
QUALITY OF THE FLUSH	☆	☆	☆	☆	☆
TOILET PAPER	☆	☆	☆	☆	☆

OVERALL EXPERIENCE:

☐ BEST SEAT IN THE HOUSE   ★ ★ ★ ★ ★
☐ WOULD POOP HERE AGAIN   ★ ★ ★ ★
☐ SHIT GOT REAL   ★ ★ ★
☐ SAME SHIT DIFFERENT HOUSE   ★ ★
☐ THINGS JUST DIDN'T COME OUT RIGHT ★

THOUGHTS/MESSAGES: _____

_____

Welcome! PLEASE SEAT YOURSELF AND ENJOY YOUR VISIT!

NAME: _____ DATE: _____ TIME: _____ DURATION OF VISIT: _____

HRS   MIN   SEC

PURPOSE FOR VISIT: 🧻 #1   🧻 #2   🧻 OTHER: _____   SUCCESS? 🧻 YES 🧻 NO

FAVORITE EUPHEMISM FOR PERFORMING #1:

FAVORITE RESTROOM GRAFFITI OR YOUR ORIGNAL DOODLE:

FAVORITE EUPHEMISM FOR PERFORMING #2:

WHILE YOU WERE HERE, DID YOU:
- ☐ TEXT SOMEONE
- ☐ MAKE A PHONE CALL
- ☐ EMAIL
- ☐ CHECK SOCIAL MEDIA
- ☐ TAKE A SELFIE
- ☐ LOOK IN THE MEDICINE CABINET
- ☐ CHECK YOUR TEETH
- ☐ CHECK OUT YOUR BUTT
- ☐ CHECK YOUR FLY
- ☐ READ
- ☐ FIX YOUR HAIR
- ☐ TAKE SOME EXTRA "ME TIME"
- ☐ TALK TO YOURSELF
- ☐ CONDUCT BUSINESS OTHER THAN YOUR "BUSINESS." CARE TO SHARE?

FAVORITE NAME FOR THIS ROOM:
- ☐ BATHROOM
- ☐ TOILET
- ☐ POWDER ROOM
- ☐ LAVATORY
- ☐ SHITTER
- ☐ LOO
- ☐ LITTLE GIRLS ROOM
- ☐ LITTLE BOYS ROOM
- ☐ COMFORT STATION
- ☐ OTHER: _____

- ☐ JOHN
- ☐ CAN
- ☐ HEAD
- ☐ POTTY
- ☐ CRAPPER
- ☐ WC

RATINGS:

	1	2	3	4	5
CLEANLINESS	☆	☆	☆	☆	☆
AMBIENCE	☆	☆	☆	☆	☆
AMENITIES	☆	☆	☆	☆	☆
SOUND PROOFING	☆	☆	☆	☆	☆
QUALITY OF THE FLUSH	☆	☆	☆	☆	☆
TOILET PAPER	☆	☆	☆	☆	☆

OVERALL EXPERIENCE:
- ☐ BEST SEAT IN THE HOUSE ★ ★ ★ ★ ★
- ☐ WOULD POOP HERE AGAIN ★ ★ ★ ★
- ☐ SHIT GOT REAL ★ ★ ★
- ☐ SAME SHIT DIFFERENT HOUSE ★ ★
- ☐ THINGS JUST DIDN'T COME OUT RIGHT ★

THOUGHTS/MESSAGES: _____
_____
_____

Welcome! PLEASE SEAT YOURSELF AND ENJOY YOUR VISIT!

NAME: _____ DATE: _____ TIME: _____ DURATION OF VISIT: _____
HRS MIN SEC

PURPOSE FOR VISIT: ☐ #1 ☐ #2 ☐ OTHER: _____ SUCCESS? ☐ YES ☐ NO

FAVORITE EUPHEMISM FOR PERFORMING #1:

FAVORITE RESTROOM GRAFFITI OR YOUR ORIGNAL DOODLE:

FAVORITE EUPHEMISM FOR PERFORMING #2:

WHILE YOU WERE HERE, DID YOU:
☐ TEXT SOMEONE
☐ MAKE A PHONE CALL
☐ EMAIL
☐ CHECK SOCIAL MEDIA
☐ TAKE A SELFIE
☐ LOOK IN THE MEDICINE CABINET
☐ CHECK YOUR TEETH
☐ CHECK OUT YOUR BUTT
☐ CHECK YOUR FLY
☐ READ
☐ FIX YOUR HAIR
☐ TAKE SOME EXTRA "ME TIME"
☐ TALK TO YOURSELF
☐ CONDUCT BUSINESS OTHER THAN YOUR "BUSINESS." CARE TO SHARE?

FAVORITE NAME FOR THIS ROOM:
☐ BATHROOM   ☐ JOHN
☐ TOILET   ☐ CAN
☐ POWDER ROOM   ☐ HEAD
☐ LAVATORY   ☐ POTTY
☐ SHITTER   ☐ CRAPPER
☐ LOO   ☐ WC
☐ LITTLE GIRLS ROOM
☐ LITTLE BOYS ROOM
☐ COMFORT STATION
☐ OTHER: _____

_____

RATINGS:
	1	2	3	4	5
CLEANLINESS	☆	☆	☆	☆	☆
AMBIENCE	☆	☆	☆	☆	☆
AMENITIES	☆	☆	☆	☆	☆
SOUND PROOFING	☆	☆	☆	☆	☆
QUALITY OF THE FLUSH	☆	☆	☆	☆	☆
TOILET PAPER	☆	☆	☆	☆	☆

OVERALL EXPERIENCE:
☐ BEST SEAT IN THE HOUSE   ★ ★ ★ ★ ★
☐ WOULD POOP HERE AGAIN   ★ ★ ★ ★
☐ SHIT GOT REAL   ★ ★ ★
☐ SAME SHIT DIFFERENT HOUSE ★ ★
☐ THINGS JUST DIDN'T COME OUT RIGHT ★

THOUGHTS/MESSAGES: _____

Welcome! PLEASE SEAT YOURSELF AND ENJOY YOUR VISIT!

NAME: _____ DATE: _____ TIME: _____ DURATION OF VISIT: _____

HRS   MIN   SEC

PURPOSE FOR VISIT: ⬚ #1 ⬚ #2 ⬚ OTHER: _____ SUCCESS? ⬚ YES ⬚ NO

FAVORITE EUPHEMISM FOR PERFORMING #1:

FAVORITE RESTROOM GRAFFITI OR YOUR ORIGNAL DOODLE:

FAVORITE EUPHEMISM FOR PERFORMING #2:

WHILE YOU WERE HERE, DID YOU:
- ☐ TEXT SOMEONE
- ☐ MAKE A PHONE CALL
- ☐ EMAIL
- ☐ CHECK SOCIAL MEDIA
- ☐ TAKE A SELFIE
- ☐ LOOK IN THE MEDICINE CABINET
- ☐ CHECK YOUR TEETH
- ☐ CHECK OUT YOUR BUTT
- ☐ CHECK YOUR FLY
- ☐ READ
- ☐ FIX YOUR HAIR
- ☐ TAKE SOME EXTRA "ME TIME"
- ☐ TALK TO YOURSELF
- ☐ CONDUCT BUSINESS OTHER THAN YOUR "BUSINESS." CARE TO SHARE?
_____

FAVORITE NAME FOR THIS ROOM:
- ☐ BATHROOM
- ☐ TOILET
- ☐ POWDER ROOM
- ☐ LAVATORY
- ☐ SHITTER
- ☐ LOO
- ☐ LITTLE GIRLS ROOM
- ☐ LITTLE BOYS ROOM
- ☐ COMFORT STATION
- ☐ OTHER: _____
- ☐ JOHN
- ☐ CAN
- ☐ HEAD
- ☐ POTTY
- ☐ CRAPPER
- ☐ WC

_____

THOUGHTS/MESSAGES: _____
_____
_____

RATINGS:	1	2	3	4	5
CLEANLINESS	☆	☆	☆	☆	☆
AMBIENCE	☆	☆	☆	☆	☆
AMENITIES	☆	☆	☆	☆	☆
SOUND PROOFING	☆	☆	☆	☆	☆
QUALITY OF THE FLUSH	☆	☆	☆	☆	☆
TOILET PAPER	☆	☆	☆	☆	☆

OVERALL EXPERIENCE:
- ☐ BEST SEAT IN THE HOUSE ★ ★ ★ ★ ★
- ☐ WOULD POOP HERE AGAIN ★ ★ ★ ★
- ☐ SHIT GOT REAL ★ ★ ★
- ☐ SAME SHIT DIFFERENT HOUSE ★ ★
- ☐ THINGS JUST DIDN'T COME OUT RIGHT ★

Welcome! PLEASE SEAT YOURSELF AND ENJOY YOUR VISIT!

NAME: _____ DATE: _____ TIME: _____ DURATION OF VISIT: _____
                                                                                  HRS   MIN   SEC

PURPOSE FOR VISIT: ☐ #1 ☐ #2 ☐ OTHER: _____ SUCCESS? ☐ YES ☐ NO

FAVORITE EUPHEMISM FOR PERFORMING #1:

FAVORITE EUPHEMISM FOR PERFORMING #2:

FAVORITE RESTROOM GRAFFITI OR YOUR ORIGNAL DOODLE:

WHILE YOU WERE HERE, DID YOU:
- ☐ TEXT SOMEONE
- ☐ MAKE A PHONE CALL
- ☐ EMAIL
- ☐ CHECK SOCIAL MEDIA
- ☐ TAKE A SELFIE
- ☐ LOOK IN THE MEDICINE CABINET
- ☐ CHECK YOUR TEETH
- ☐ CHECK OUT YOUR BUTT
- ☐ CHECK YOUR FLY
- ☐ READ
- ☐ FIX YOUR HAIR
- ☐ TAKE SOME EXTRA "ME TIME"
- ☐ TALK TO YOURSELF
- ☐ CONDUCT BUSINESS OTHER THAN YOUR "BUSINESS." CARE TO SHARE?

FAVORITE NAME FOR THIS ROOM:
- ☐ BATHROOM
- ☐ TOILET
- ☐ POWDER ROOM
- ☐ LAVATORY
- ☐ SHITTER
- ☐ LOO
- ☐ LITTLE GIRLS ROOM
- ☐ LITTLE BOYS ROOM
- ☐ COMFORT STATION
- ☐ OTHER: _____
- ☐ JOHN
- ☐ CAN
- ☐ HEAD
- ☐ POTTY
- ☐ CRAPPER
- ☐ WC

RATINGS:
	1	2	3	4	5
CLEANLINESS	☆	☆	☆	☆	☆
AMBIENCE	☆	☆	☆	☆	☆
AMENITIES	☆	☆	☆	☆	☆
SOUND PROOFING	☆	☆	☆	☆	☆
QUALITY OF THE FLUSH	☆	☆	☆	☆	☆
TOILET PAPER	☆	☆	☆	☆	☆

OVERALL EXPERIENCE:
- ☐ BEST SEAT IN THE HOUSE ★ ★ ★ ★ ★
- ☐ WOULD POOP HERE AGAIN ★ ★ ★ ★
- ☐ SHIT GOT REAL ★ ★ ★
- ☐ SAME SHIT DIFFERENT HOUSE ★ ★
- ☐ THINGS JUST DIDN'T COME OUT RIGHT ★

THOUGHTS/MESSAGES: _____
_____
_____

Welcome! PLEASE SEAT YOURSELF AND ENJOY YOUR VISIT!

NAME: _____ DATE: _____ TIME: _____ DURATION OF VISIT: _____
                                                                                      HRS   MIN   SEC

PURPOSE FOR VISIT: 🧻 #1   🧻 #2   🧻 OTHER: _____   SUCCESS? 🧻 YES 🧻 NO

FAVORITE EUPHEMISM FOR PERFORMING #1:

FAVORITE RESTROOM GRAFFITI OR YOUR ORIGNAL DOODLE:

FAVORITE EUPHEMISM FOR PERFORMING #2:

WHILE YOU WERE HERE, DID YOU:
- ☐ TEXT SOMEONE
- ☐ MAKE A PHONE CALL
- ☐ EMAIL
- ☐ CHECK SOCIAL MEDIA
- ☐ TAKE A SELFIE
- ☐ LOOK IN THE MEDICINE CABINET
- ☐ CHECK YOUR TEETH
- ☐ CHECK OUT YOUR BUTT
- ☐ CHECK YOUR FLY
- ☐ READ
- ☐ FIX YOUR HAIR
- ☐ TAKE SOME EXTRA "ME TIME"
- ☐ TALK TO YOURSELF
- ☐ CONDUCT BUSINESS OTHER THAN YOUR "BUSINESS." CARE TO SHARE?

FAVORITE NAME FOR THIS ROOM:
- ☐ BATHROOM
- ☐ TOILET
- ☐ POWDER ROOM
- ☐ LAVATORY
- ☐ SHITTER
- ☐ LOO
- ☐ LITTLE GIRLS ROOM
- ☐ LITTLE BOYS ROOM
- ☐ COMFORT STATION
- ☐ OTHER: _____

- ☐ JOHN
- ☐ CAN
- ☐ HEAD
- ☐ POTTY
- ☐ CRAPPER
- ☐ WC

RATINGS:
	1 2 3 4 5
CLEANLINESS	☆ ☆ ☆ ☆ ☆
AMBIENCE	☆ ☆ ☆ ☆ ☆
AMENITIES	☆ ☆ ☆ ☆ ☆
SOUND PROOFING	☆ ☆ ☆ ☆ ☆
QUALITY OF THE FLUSH	☆ ☆ ☆ ☆ ☆
TOILET PAPER	☆ ☆ ☆ ☆ ☆

OVERALL EXPERIENCE:
- ☐ BEST SEAT IN THE HOUSE ★ ★ ★ ★ ★
- ☐ WOULD POOP HERE AGAIN ★ ★ ★ ★
- ☐ SHIT GOT REAL ★ ★ ★
- ☐ SAME SHIT DIFFERENT HOUSE ★ ★
- ☐ THINGS JUST DIDN'T COME OUT RIGHT ★

THOUGHTS/MESSAGES: _____

Welcome! PLEASE SEAT YOURSELF AND ENJOY YOUR VISIT!

NAME: _____ DATE: _____ TIME: _____ DURATION OF VISIT: _____
HRS   MIN   SEC

PURPOSE FOR VISIT: ☐ #1 ☐ #2 ☐ OTHER: _____ SUCCESS? ☐ YES ☐ NO

FAVORITE EUPHEMISM FOR PERFORMING #1:

FAVORITE RESTROOM GRAFFITI OR YOUR ORIGNAL DOODLE:

FAVORITE EUPHEMISM FOR PERFORMING #2:

WHILE YOU WERE HERE, DID YOU:
- ☐ TEXT SOMEONE
- ☐ MAKE A PHONE CALL
- ☐ EMAIL
- ☐ CHECK SOCIAL MEDIA
- ☐ TAKE A SELFIE
- ☐ LOOK IN THE MEDICINE CABINET
- ☐ CHECK YOUR TEETH
- ☐ CHECK OUT YOUR BUTT
- ☐ CHECK YOUR FLY
- ☐ READ
- ☐ FIX YOUR HAIR
- ☐ TAKE SOME EXTRA "ME TIME"
- ☐ TALK TO YOURSELF
- ☐ CONDUCT BUSINESS OTHER THAN YOUR "BUSINESS." CARE TO SHARE?

FAVORITE NAME FOR THIS ROOM:
- ☐ BATHROOM
- ☐ TOILET
- ☐ POWDER ROOM
- ☐ LAVATORY
- ☐ SHITTER
- ☐ LOO
- ☐ LITTLE GIRLS ROOM
- ☐ LITTLE BOYS ROOM
- ☐ COMFORT STATION
- ☐ OTHER: _____
- ☐ JOHN
- ☐ CAN
- ☐ HEAD
- ☐ POTTY
- ☐ CRAPPER
- ☐ WC

RATINGS:
	1	2	3	4	5
CLEANLINESS	☆	☆	☆	☆	☆
AMBIENCE	☆	☆	☆	☆	☆
AMENITIES	☆	☆	☆	☆	☆
SOUND PROOFING	☆	☆	☆	☆	☆
QUALITY OF THE FLUSH	☆	☆	☆	☆	☆
TOILET PAPER	☆	☆	☆	☆	☆

OVERALL EXPERIENCE:
- ☐ BEST SEAT IN THE HOUSE ★★★★★
- ☐ WOULD POOP HERE AGAIN ★★★★
- ☐ SHIT GOT REAL ★★★
- ☐ SAME SHIT DIFFERENT HOUSE ★★
- ☐ THINGS JUST DIDN'T COME OUT RIGHT ★

THOUGHTS/MESSAGES: _____

Welcome! PLEASE SEAT YOURSELF AND ENJOY YOUR VISIT!

NAME: _____ DATE: _____ TIME: _____ DURATION OF VISIT: _____
HRS   MIN   SEC

PURPOSE FOR VISIT: ▢ #1   ▢ #2   ▢ OTHER: _____   SUCCESS? ▢ YES ▢ NO

FAVORITE EUPHEMISM FOR PERFORMING #1:

FAVORITE RESTROOM GRAFFITI OR YOUR ORIGNAL DOODLE:

FAVORITE EUPHEMISM FOR PERFORMING #2:

WHILE YOU WERE HERE, DID YOU:
- ☐ TEXT SOMEONE
- ☐ MAKE A PHONE CALL
- ☐ EMAIL
- ☐ CHECK SOCIAL MEDIA
- ☐ TAKE A SELFIE
- ☐ LOOK IN THE MEDICINE CABINET
- ☐ CHECK YOUR TEETH
- ☐ CHECK OUT YOUR BUTT
- ☐ CHECK YOUR FLY
- ☐ READ
- ☐ FIX YOUR HAIR
- ☐ TAKE SOME EXTRA "ME TIME"
- ☐ TALK TO YOURSELF
- ☐ CONDUCT BUSINESS OTHER THAN YOUR "BUSINESS." CARE TO SHARE?
_____

FAVORITE NAME FOR THIS ROOM:
- ☐ BATHROOM
- ☐ TOILET
- ☐ POWDER ROOM
- ☐ LAVATORY
- ☐ SHITTER
- ☐ LOO
- ☐ LITTLE GIRLS ROOM
- ☐ LITTLE BOYS ROOM
- ☐ COMFORT STATION
- ☐ OTHER: _____
- ☐ JOHN
- ☐ CAN
- ☐ HEAD
- ☐ POTTY
- ☐ CRAPPER
- ☐ WC

_____

THOUGHTS/MESSAGES: _____
_____
_____

RATINGS: 1 2 3 4 5
CLEANLINESS   ☆ ☆ ☆ ☆ ☆
AMBIENCE   ☆ ☆ ☆ ☆ ☆
AMENITIES   ☆ ☆ ☆ ☆ ☆
SOUND PROOFING   ☆ ☆ ☆ ☆ ☆
QUALITY OF THE FLUSH ☆ ☆ ☆ ☆ ☆
TOILET PAPER   ☆ ☆ ☆ ☆ ☆

OVERALL EXPERIENCE:
- ☐ BEST SEAT IN THE HOUSE   ★ ★ ★ ★ ★
- ☐ WOULD POOP HERE AGAIN   ★ ★ ★ ★
- ☐ SHIT GOT REAL   ★ ★ ★
- ☐ SAME SHIT DIFFERENT HOUSE   ★ ★
- ☐ THINGS JUST DIDN'T COME OUT RIGHT ★

Welcome! PLEASE SEAT YOURSELF AND ENJOY YOUR VISIT!

NAME: _____ DATE: _____ TIME: _____ DURATION OF VISIT: _____

HRS   MIN   SEC

PURPOSE FOR VISIT: 🧻 #1 🧻 #2 🧻 OTHER: _____ SUCCESS? 🧻 YES 🧻 NO

FAVORITE EUPHEMISM FOR PERFORMING #1:   FAVORITE RESTROOM GRAFFITI OR YOUR ORIGNAL DOODLE:

FAVORITE EUPHEMISM FOR PERFORMING #2:

WHILE YOU WERE HERE, DID YOU:
- ☐ TEXT SOMEONE
- ☐ MAKE A PHONE CALL
- ☐ EMAIL
- ☐ CHECK SOCIAL MEDIA
- ☐ TAKE A SELFIE
- ☐ LOOK IN THE MEDICINE CABINET
- ☐ CHECK YOUR TEETH
- ☐ CHECK OUT YOUR BUTT
- ☐ CHECK YOUR FLY
- ☐ READ
- ☐ FIX YOUR HAIR
- ☐ TAKE SOME EXTRA "ME TIME"
- ☐ TALK TO YOURSELF
- ☐ CONDUCT BUSINESS OTHER THAN YOUR "BUSINESS." CARE TO SHARE?

FAVORITE NAME FOR THIS ROOM:
- ☐ BATHROOM
- ☐ TOILET
- ☐ POWDER ROOM
- ☐ LAVATORY
- ☐ SHITTER
- ☐ LOO
- ☐ LITTLE GIRLS ROOM
- ☐ LITTLE BOYS ROOM
- ☐ COMFORT STATION
- ☐ OTHER: _____

- ☐ JOHN
- ☐ CAN
- ☐ HEAD
- ☐ POTTY
- ☐ CRAPPER
- ☐ WC

_____

RATINGS:

	1	2	3	4	5
CLEANLINESS	☆	☆	☆	☆	☆
AMBIENCE	☆	☆	☆	☆	☆
AMENITIES	☆	☆	☆	☆	☆
SOUND PROOFING	☆	☆	☆	☆	☆
QUALITY OF THE FLUSH	☆	☆	☆	☆	☆
TOILET PAPER	☆	☆	☆	☆	☆

OVERALL EXPERIENCE:
- ☐ BEST SEAT IN THE HOUSE ★★★★★
- ☐ WOULD POOP HERE AGAIN ★★★★
- ☐ SHIT GOT REAL ★★★
- ☐ SAME SHIT DIFFERENT HOUSE ★★
- ☐ THINGS JUST DIDN'T COME OUT RIGHT ★

THOUGHTS/MESSAGES: _____

_____

_____

 *Welcome!* PLEASE SEAT YOURSELF AND ENJOY YOUR VISIT!

NAME: _____ DATE: _____ TIME: _____ DURATION OF VISIT: _____
HRS   MIN   SEC

PURPOSE FOR VISIT: ⬜ #1 ⬜ #2 ⬜ OTHER: _____ SUCCESS? ⬜ YES ⬜ NO

FAVORITE EUPHEMISM FOR PERFORMING #1:

FAVORITE RESTROOM GRAFFITI OR YOUR ORIGNAL DOODLE:

FAVORITE EUPHEMISM FOR PERFORMING #2:

WHILE YOU WERE HERE, DID YOU:
- ⬜ TEXT SOMEONE
- ⬜ MAKE A PHONE CALL
- ⬜ EMAIL
- ⬜ CHECK SOCIAL MEDIA
- ⬜ TAKE A SELFIE
- ⬜ LOOK IN THE MEDICINE CABINET
- ⬜ CHECK YOUR TEETH
- ⬜ CHECK OUT YOUR BUTT
- ⬜ CHECK YOUR FLY
- ⬜ READ
- ⬜ FIX YOUR HAIR
- ⬜ TAKE SOME EXTRA "ME TIME"
- ⬜ TALK TO YOURSELF
- ⬜ CONDUCT BUSINESS OTHER THAN YOUR "BUSINESS." CARE TO SHARE?
_____

FAVORITE NAME FOR THIS ROOM:
- ⬜ BATHROOM
- ⬜ TOILET
- ⬜ POWDER ROOM
- ⬜ LAVATORY
- ⬜ SHITTER
- ⬜ LOO
- ⬜ LITTLE GIRLS ROOM
- ⬜ LITTLE BOYS ROOM
- ⬜ COMFORT STATION
- ⬜ OTHER: _____
- ⬜ JOHN
- ⬜ CAN
- ⬜ HEAD
- ⬜ POTTY
- ⬜ CRAPPER
- ⬜ WC

_____

THOUGHTS/MESSAGES: _____
_____
_____

RATINGS:

	1	2	3	4	5
CLEANLINESS	☆	☆	☆	☆	☆
AMBIENCE	☆	☆	☆	☆	☆
AMENITIES	☆	☆	☆	☆	☆
SOUND PROOFING	☆	☆	☆	☆	☆
QUALITY OF THE FLUSH	☆	☆	☆	☆	☆
TOILET PAPER	☆	☆	☆	☆	☆

OVERALL EXPERIENCE:
- ⬜ BEST SEAT IN THE HOUSE ★ ★ ★ ★ ★
- ⬜ WOULD POOP HERE AGAIN ★ ★ ★ ★
- ⬜ SHIT GOT REAL ★ ★ ★
- ⬜ SAME SHIT DIFFERENT HOUSE ★ ★
- ⬜ THINGS JUST DIDN'T COME OUT RIGHT ★

Welcome! PLEASE SEAT YOURSELF AND ENJOY YOUR VISIT!

NAME: _____ DATE: _____ TIME: _____ DURATION OF VISIT: _____
                                                                    HRS   MIN   SEC

PURPOSE FOR VISIT: ☐ #1 ☐ #2 ☐ OTHER: _____ SUCCESS? ☐ YES ☐ NO

FAVORITE EUPHEMISM FOR PERFORMING #1:   FAVORITE RESTROOM GRAFFITI OR YOUR ORIGNAL DOODLE:

FAVORITE EUPHEMISM FOR PERFORMING #2:

WHILE YOU WERE HERE, DID YOU:
- ☐ TEXT SOMEONE
- ☐ MAKE A PHONE CALL
- ☐ EMAIL
- ☐ CHECK SOCIAL MEDIA
- ☐ TAKE A SELFIE
- ☐ LOOK IN THE MEDICINE CABINET
- ☐ CHECK YOUR TEETH
- ☐ CHECK OUT YOUR BUTT
- ☐ CHECK YOUR FLY
- ☐ READ
- ☐ FIX YOUR HAIR
- ☐ TAKE SOME EXTRA "ME TIME"
- ☐ TALK TO YOURSELF
- ☐ CONDUCT BUSINESS OTHER THAN YOUR "BUSINESS." CARE TO SHARE?

FAVORITE NAME FOR THIS ROOM:
- ☐ BATHROOM
- ☐ TOILET
- ☐ POWDER ROOM
- ☐ LAVATORY
- ☐ SHITTER
- ☐ LOO
- ☐ LITTLE GIRLS ROOM
- ☐ LITTLE BOYS ROOM
- ☐ COMFORT STATION
- ☐ JOHN
- ☐ CAN
- ☐ HEAD
- ☐ POTTY
- ☐ CRAPPER
- ☐ WC
- ☐ OTHER: _____

_____

RATINGS: 1 2 3 4 5
CLEANLINESS   ☆ ☆ ☆ ☆ ☆
AMBIENCE   ☆ ☆ ☆ ☆ ☆
AMENITIES   ☆ ☆ ☆ ☆ ☆
SOUND PROOFING   ☆ ☆ ☆ ☆ ☆
QUALITY OF THE FLUSH ☆ ☆ ☆ ☆ ☆
TOILET PAPER   ☆ ☆ ☆ ☆ ☆

OVERALL EXPERIENCE:
- ☐ BEST SEAT IN THE HOUSE   ★ ★ ★ ★ ★
- ☐ WOULD POOP HERE AGAIN   ★ ★ ★ ★
- ☐ SHIT GOT REAL   ★ ★ ★
- ☐ SAME SHIT DIFFERENT HOUSE   ★ ★
- ☐ THINGS JUST DIDN'T COME OUT RIGHT   ★

THOUGHTS/MESSAGES: _____
_____
_____

Welcome! PLEASE SEAT YOURSELF AND ENJOY YOUR VISIT!

NAME: _____ DATE: _____ TIME: _____ DURATION OF VISIT: _____
HRS   MIN   SEC

PURPOSE FOR VISIT: 🧻 #1   🧻 #2   🧻 OTHER: _____   SUCCESS? 🧻 YES 🧻 NO

FAVORITE EUPHEMISM FOR PERFORMING #1:

FAVORITE RESTROOM GRAFFITI OR YOUR ORIGNAL DOODLE:

FAVORITE EUPHEMISM FOR PERFORMING #2:

WHILE YOU WERE HERE, DID YOU:
- ☐ TEXT SOMEONE
- ☐ MAKE A PHONE CALL
- ☐ EMAIL
- ☐ CHECK SOCIAL MEDIA
- ☐ TAKE A SELFIE
- ☐ LOOK IN THE MEDICINE CABINET
- ☐ CHECK YOUR TEETH
- ☐ CHECK OUT YOUR BUTT
- ☐ CHECK YOUR FLY
- ☐ READ
- ☐ FIX YOUR HAIR
- ☐ TAKE SOME EXTRA "ME TIME"
- ☐ TALK TO YOURSELF
- ☐ CONDUCT BUSINESS OTHER THAN YOUR "BUSINESS." CARE TO SHARE?
  _____

FAVORITE NAME FOR THIS ROOM:
- ☐ BATHROOM
- ☐ TOILET
- ☐ POWDER ROOM
- ☐ LAVATORY
- ☐ SHITTER
- ☐ LOO
- ☐ LITTLE GIRLS ROOM
- ☐ LITTLE BOYS ROOM
- ☐ COMFORT STATION
- ☐ OTHER: _____
- ☐ JOHN
- ☐ CAN
- ☐ HEAD
- ☐ POTTY
- ☐ CRAPPER
- ☐ WC

_____

THOUGHTS/MESSAGES: _____
_____
_____

RATINGS:

	1	2	3	4	5
CLEANLINESS	☆	☆	☆	☆	☆
AMBIENCE	☆	☆	☆	☆	☆
AMENITIES	☆	☆	☆	☆	☆
SOUND PROOFING	☆	☆	☆	☆	☆
QUALITY OF THE FLUSH	☆	☆	☆	☆	☆
TOILET PAPER	☆	☆	☆	☆	☆

OVERALL EXPERIENCE:
- ☐ BEST SEAT IN THE HOUSE ★ ★ ★ ★ ★
- ☐ WOULD POOP HERE AGAIN ★ ★ ★ ★
- ☐ SHIT GOT REAL ★ ★ ★
- ☐ SAME SHIT DIFFERENT HOUSE ★ ★
- ☐ THINGS JUST DIDN'T COME OUT RIGHT ★

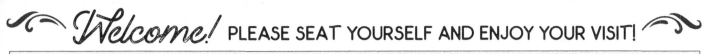

Welcome! PLEASE SEAT YOURSELF AND ENJOY YOUR VISIT!

NAME: _____ DATE: _____ TIME: _____ DURATION OF VISIT: _____

HRS MIN SEC

PURPOSE FOR VISIT: 🧻 #1 🧻 #2 🧻 OTHER: _____ SUCCESS? 🧻 YES 🧻 NO

FAVORITE EUPHEMISM FOR PERFORMING #1:

FAVORITE RESTROOM GRAFFITI OR YOUR ORIGNAL DOODLE:

FAVORITE EUPHEMISM FOR PERFORMING #2:

WHILE YOU WERE HERE, DID YOU:
- ☐ TEXT SOMEONE
- ☐ MAKE A PHONE CALL
- ☐ EMAIL
- ☐ CHECK SOCIAL MEDIA
- ☐ TAKE A SELFIE
- ☐ LOOK IN THE MEDICINE CABINET
- ☐ CHECK YOUR TEETH
- ☐ CHECK OUT YOUR BUTT
- ☐ CHECK YOUR FLY
- ☐ READ
- ☐ FIX YOUR HAIR
- ☐ TAKE SOME EXTRA "ME TIME"
- ☐ TALK TO YOURSELF
- ☐ CONDUCT BUSINESS OTHER THAN YOUR "BUSINESS." CARE TO SHARE?
_____

FAVORITE NAME FOR THIS ROOM:
- ☐ BATHROOM
- ☐ TOILET
- ☐ POWDER ROOM
- ☐ LAVATORY
- ☐ SHITTER
- ☐ LOO
- ☐ LITTLE GIRLS ROOM
- ☐ LITTLE BOYS ROOM
- ☐ COMFORT STATION
- ☐ OTHER: _____
- ☐ JOHN
- ☐ CAN
- ☐ HEAD
- ☐ POTTY
- ☐ CRAPPER
- ☐ WC

RATINGS:

	1	2	3	4	5
CLEANLINESS	☆	☆	☆	☆	☆
AMBIENCE	☆	☆	☆	☆	☆
AMENITIES	☆	☆	☆	☆	☆
SOUND PROOFING	☆	☆	☆	☆	☆
QUALITY OF THE FLUSH	☆	☆	☆	☆	☆
TOILET PAPER	☆	☆	☆	☆	☆

OVERALL EXPERIENCE:
- ☐ BEST SEAT IN THE HOUSE ★ ★ ★ ★ ★
- ☐ WOULD POOP HERE AGAIN ★ ★ ★ ★
- ☐ SHIT GOT REAL ★ ★ ★
- ☐ SAME SHIT DIFFERENT HOUSE ★ ★
- ☐ THINGS JUST DIDN'T COME OUT RIGHT ★

THOUGHTS/MESSAGES: _____
_____
_____

Welcome! PLEASE SEAT YOURSELF AND ENJOY YOUR VISIT!

NAME: _____ DATE: _____ TIME: _____ DURATION OF VISIT: _____
HRS   MIN   SEC

PURPOSE FOR VISIT: ☐ #1 ☐ #2 ☐ OTHER: _____ SUCCESS? ☐ YES ☐ NO

FAVORITE EUPHEMISM FOR PERFORMING #1:   FAVORITE RESTROOM GRAFFITI OR YOUR ORIGNAL DOODLE:

FAVORITE EUPHEMISM FOR PERFORMING #2:

WHILE YOU WERE HERE, DID YOU:
- ☐ TEXT SOMEONE
- ☐ MAKE A PHONE CALL
- ☐ EMAIL
- ☐ CHECK SOCIAL MEDIA
- ☐ TAKE A SELFIE
- ☐ LOOK IN THE MEDICINE CABINET
- ☐ CHECK YOUR TEETH
- ☐ CHECK OUT YOUR BUTT
- ☐ CHECK YOUR FLY
- ☐ READ
- ☐ FIX YOUR HAIR
- ☐ TAKE SOME EXTRA "ME TIME"
- ☐ TALK TO YOURSELF
- ☐ CONDUCT BUSINESS OTHER THAN YOUR "BUSINESS." CARE TO SHARE?
  _____

FAVORITE NAME FOR THIS ROOM:
- ☐ BATHROOM
- ☐ TOILET
- ☐ POWDER ROOM
- ☐ LAVATORY
- ☐ SHITTER
- ☐ LOO
- ☐ LITTLE GIRLS ROOM
- ☐ LITTLE BOYS ROOM
- ☐ COMFORT STATION
- ☐ OTHER: _____

- ☐ JOHN
- ☐ CAN
- ☐ HEAD
- ☐ POTTY
- ☐ CRAPPER
- ☐ WC

RATINGS: 1 2 3 4 5

	1	2	3	4	5
CLEANLINESS	☆	☆	☆	☆	☆
AMBIENCE	☆	☆	☆	☆	☆
AMENITIES	☆	☆	☆	☆	☆
SOUND PROOFING	☆	☆	☆	☆	☆
QUALITY OF THE FLUSH	☆	☆	☆	☆	☆
TOILET PAPER	☆	☆	☆	☆	☆

OVERALL EXPERIENCE:
- ☐ BEST SEAT IN THE HOUSE ★ ★ ★ ★ ★
- ☐ WOULD POOP HERE AGAIN ★ ★ ★ ★
- ☐ SHIT GOT REAL ★ ★ ★
- ☐ SAME SHIT DIFFERENT HOUSE ★ ★
- ☐ THINGS JUST DIDN'T COME OUT RIGHT ★

THOUGHTS/MESSAGES: _____
_____
_____

Welcome! PLEASE SEAT YOURSELF AND ENJOY YOUR VISIT!

NAME: _____ DATE: _____ TIME: _____ DURATION OF VISIT: _____
                                                                              HRS   MIN   SEC

PURPOSE FOR VISIT: ▢ #1 ▢ #2 ▢ OTHER: _____ SUCCESS? ▢ YES ▢ NO

FAVORITE EUPHEMISM FOR PERFORMING #1:

FAVORITE RESTROOM GRAFFITI OR YOUR ORIGNAL DOODLE:

FAVORITE EUPHEMISM FOR PERFORMING #2:

WHILE YOU WERE HERE, DID YOU:
- ☐ TEXT SOMEONE
- ☐ MAKE A PHONE CALL
- ☐ EMAIL
- ☐ CHECK SOCIAL MEDIA
- ☐ TAKE A SELFIE
- ☐ LOOK IN THE MEDICINE CABINET
- ☐ CHECK YOUR TEETH
- ☐ CHECK OUT YOUR BUTT
- ☐ CHECK YOUR FLY
- ☐ READ
- ☐ FIX YOUR HAIR
- ☐ TAKE SOME EXTRA "ME TIME"
- ☐ TALK TO YOURSELF
- ☐ CONDUCT BUSINESS OTHER THAN YOUR "BUSINESS." CARE TO SHARE?

FAVORITE NAME FOR THIS ROOM:
- ☐ BATHROOM
- ☐ TOILET
- ☐ POWDER ROOM
- ☐ LAVATORY
- ☐ SHITTER
- ☐ LOO
- ☐ LITTLE GIRLS ROOM
- ☐ LITTLE BOYS ROOM
- ☐ COMFORT STATION
- ☐ OTHER: _____
- ☐ JOHN
- ☐ CAN
- ☐ HEAD
- ☐ POTTY
- ☐ CRAPPER
- ☐ WC

RATINGS: 1 2 3 4 5
CLEANLINESS   ☆ ☆ ☆ ☆ ☆
AMBIENCE   ☆ ☆ ☆ ☆ ☆
AMENITIES   ☆ ☆ ☆ ☆ ☆
SOUND PROOFING   ☆ ☆ ☆ ☆ ☆
QUALITY OF THE FLUSH ☆ ☆ ☆ ☆ ☆
TOILET PAPER   ☆ ☆ ☆ ☆ ☆

OVERALL EXPERIENCE:
- ☐ BEST SEAT IN THE HOUSE ★ ★ ★ ★ ★
- ☐ WOULD POOP HERE AGAIN ★ ★ ★ ★
- ☐ SHIT GOT REAL ★ ★ ★
- ☐ SAME SHIT DIFFERENT HOUSE ★ ★
- ☐ THINGS JUST DIDN'T COME OUT RIGHT ★

THOUGHTS/MESSAGES: _____

Welcome! PLEASE SEAT YOURSELF AND ENJOY YOUR VISIT!

NAME: _____ DATE: _____ TIME: _____ DURATION OF VISIT: _____
HRS   MIN   SEC

PURPOSE FOR VISIT: ☐ #1 ☐ #2 ☐ OTHER: _____ SUCCESS? ☐ YES ☐ NO

FAVORITE EUPHEMISM FOR PERFORMING #1: | FAVORITE RESTROOM GRAFFITI OR YOUR ORIGNAL DOODLE:

FAVORITE EUPHEMISM FOR PERFORMING #2:

WHILE YOU WERE HERE, DID YOU:
- ☐ TEXT SOMEONE
- ☐ MAKE A PHONE CALL
- ☐ EMAIL
- ☐ CHECK SOCIAL MEDIA
- ☐ TAKE A SELFIE
- ☐ LOOK IN THE MEDICINE CABINET
- ☐ CHECK YOUR TEETH
- ☐ CHECK OUT YOUR BUTT
- ☐ CHECK YOUR FLY
- ☐ READ
- ☐ FIX YOUR HAIR
- ☐ TAKE SOME EXTRA "ME TIME"
- ☐ TALK TO YOURSELF
- ☐ CONDUCT BUSINESS OTHER THAN YOUR "BUSINESS." CARE TO SHARE?
_____

FAVORITE NAME FOR THIS ROOM:
- ☐ BATHROOM
- ☐ TOILET
- ☐ POWDER ROOM
- ☐ LAVATORY
- ☐ SHITTER
- ☐ LOO
- ☐ LITTLE GIRLS ROOM
- ☐ LITTLE BOYS ROOM
- ☐ COMFORT STATION
- ☐ OTHER: _____

- ☐ JOHN
- ☐ CAN
- ☐ HEAD
- ☐ POTTY
- ☐ CRAPPER
- ☐ WC

_____
_____

THOUGHTS/MESSAGES: _____
_____
_____

RATINGS:
	1	2	3	4	5
CLEANLINESS	☆	☆	☆	☆	☆
AMBIENCE	☆	☆	☆	☆	☆
AMENITIES	☆	☆	☆	☆	☆
SOUND PROOFING	☆	☆	☆	☆	☆
QUALITY OF THE FLUSH	☆	☆	☆	☆	☆
TOILET PAPER	☆	☆	☆	☆	☆

OVERALL EXPERIENCE:
- ☐ BEST SEAT IN THE HOUSE ★ ★ ★ ★ ★
- ☐ WOULD POOP HERE AGAIN ★ ★ ★ ★
- ☐ SHIT GOT REAL ★ ★ ★
- ☐ SAME SHIT DIFFERENT HOUSE ★ ★
- ☐ THINGS JUST DIDN'T COME OUT RIGHT ★

Welcome! PLEASE SEAT YOURSELF AND ENJOY YOUR VISIT!

NAME: _____ DATE: _____ TIME: _____ DURATION OF VISIT: _____
                                                                              HRS   MIN   SEC

PURPOSE FOR VISIT: ☐ #1 ☐ #2 ☐ OTHER: _____ SUCCESS? ☐ YES ☐ NO

FAVORITE EUPHEMISM FOR PERFORMING #1:

FAVORITE RESTROOM GRAFFITI OR YOUR ORIGNAL DOODLE:

FAVORITE EUPHEMISM FOR PERFORMING #2:

WHILE YOU WERE HERE, DID YOU:
☐ TEXT SOMEONE
☐ MAKE A PHONE CALL
☐ EMAIL
☐ CHECK SOCIAL MEDIA
☐ TAKE A SELFIE
☐ LOOK IN THE MEDICINE CABINET
☐ CHECK YOUR TEETH
☐ CHECK OUT YOUR BUTT
☐ CHECK YOUR FLY
☐ READ
☐ FIX YOUR HAIR
☐ TAKE SOME EXTRA "ME TIME"
☐ TALK TO YOURSELF
☐ CONDUCT BUSINESS OTHER THAN YOUR "BUSINESS." CARE TO SHARE?
_____

FAVORITE NAME FOR THIS ROOM:
☐ BATHROOM   ☐ JOHN
☐ TOILET   ☐ CAN
☐ POWDER ROOM   ☐ HEAD
☐ LAVATORY   ☐ POTTY
☐ SHITTER   ☐ CRAPPER
☐ LOO   ☐ WC
☐ LITTLE GIRLS ROOM
☐ LITTLE BOYS ROOM
☐ COMFORT STATION
☐ OTHER: _____
_____
_____

RATINGS: 1 2 3 4 5
CLEANLINESS   ☆ ☆ ☆ ☆ ☆
AMBIENCE   ☆ ☆ ☆ ☆ ☆
AMENITIES   ☆ ☆ ☆ ☆ ☆
SOUND PROOFING   ☆ ☆ ☆ ☆ ☆
QUALITY OF THE FLUSH   ☆ ☆ ☆ ☆ ☆
TOILET PAPER   ☆ ☆ ☆ ☆ ☆

OVERALL EXPERIENCE:
☐ BEST SEAT IN THE HOUSE   ★ ★ ★ ★ ★
☐ WOULD POOP HERE AGAIN   ★ ★ ★ ★
☐ SHIT GOT REAL   ★ ★ ★
☐ SAME SHIT DIFFERENT HOUSE   ★ ★
☐ THINGS JUST DIDN'T COME OUT RIGHT   ★

THOUGHTS/MESSAGES: _____
_____
_____

 *Welcome!* PLEASE SEAT YOURSELF AND ENJOY YOUR VISIT!

NAME: _____ DATE: _____ TIME: _____ DURATION OF VISIT: _____
HRS   MIN   SEC

PURPOSE FOR VISIT: 🧻 #1 🧻 #2 🧻 OTHER: _____ SUCCESS? 🧻 YES 🧻 NO

FAVORITE EUPHEMISM FOR PERFORMING #1:

FAVORITE EUPHEMISM FOR PERFORMING #2:

FAVORITE RESTROOM GRAFFITI OR YOUR ORIGNAL DOODLE:

WHILE YOU WERE HERE, DID YOU:
- ☐ TEXT SOMEONE
- ☐ MAKE A PHONE CALL
- ☐ EMAIL
- ☐ CHECK SOCIAL MEDIA
- ☐ TAKE A SELFIE
- ☐ LOOK IN THE MEDICINE CABINET
- ☐ CHECK YOUR TEETH
- ☐ CHECK OUT YOUR BUTT
- ☐ CHECK YOUR FLY
- ☐ READ
- ☐ FIX YOUR HAIR
- ☐ TAKE SOME EXTRA "ME TIME"
- ☐ TALK TO YOURSELF
- ☐ CONDUCT BUSINESS OTHER THAN YOUR "BUSINESS." CARE TO SHARE?
  _____

FAVORITE NAME FOR THIS ROOM:
- ☐ BATHROOM
- ☐ TOILET
- ☐ POWDER ROOM
- ☐ LAVATORY
- ☐ SHITTER
- ☐ LOO
- ☐ LITTLE GIRLS ROOM
- ☐ LITTLE BOYS ROOM
- ☐ COMFORT STATION
- ☐ OTHER: _____
- ☐ JOHN
- ☐ CAN
- ☐ HEAD
- ☐ POTTY
- ☐ CRAPPER
- ☐ WC

_____

RATINGS:

	1	2	3	4	5
CLEANLINESS	☆	☆	☆	☆	☆
AMBIENCE	☆	☆	☆	☆	☆
AMENITIES	☆	☆	☆	☆	☆
SOUND PROOFING	☆	☆	☆	☆	☆
QUALITY OF THE FLUSH	☆	☆	☆	☆	☆
TOILET PAPER	☆	☆	☆	☆	☆

OVERALL EXPERIENCE:
- ☐ BEST SEAT IN THE HOUSE ★ ★ ★ ★ ★
- ☐ WOULD POOP HERE AGAIN ★ ★ ★ ★
- ☐ SHIT GOT REAL ★ ★ ★
- ☐ SAME SHIT DIFFERENT HOUSE ★ ★
- ☐ THINGS JUST DIDN'T COME OUT RIGHT ★

THOUGHTS/MESSAGES: _____
_____
_____

Welcome! PLEASE SEAT YOURSELF AND ENJOY YOUR VISIT!

NAME: _____ DATE: _____ TIME: _____ DURATION OF VISIT: _____
HRS   MIN   SEC

PURPOSE FOR VISIT: 🧻 #1 🧻 #2 🧻 OTHER: _____ SUCCESS? 🧻 YES 🧻 NO

FAVORITE EUPHEMISM FOR PERFORMING #1: | FAVORITE RESTROOM GRAFFITI OR YOUR ORIGNAL DOODLE:

FAVORITE EUPHEMISM FOR PERFORMING #2:

WHILE YOU WERE HERE, DID YOU:

- ☐ TEXT SOMEONE
- ☐ MAKE A PHONE CALL
- ☐ EMAIL
- ☐ CHECK SOCIAL MEDIA
- ☐ TAKE A SELFIE
- ☐ LOOK IN THE MEDICINE CABINET
- ☐ CHECK YOUR TEETH
- ☐ CHECK OUT YOUR BUTT
- ☐ CHECK YOUR FLY
- ☐ READ
- ☐ FIX YOUR HAIR
- ☐ TAKE SOME EXTRA "ME TIME"
- ☐ TALK TO YOURSELF
- ☐ CONDUCT BUSINESS OTHER THAN YOUR "BUSINESS." CARE TO SHARE?

FAVORITE NAME FOR THIS ROOM:

- ☐ BATHROOM
- ☐ TOILET
- ☐ POWDER ROOM
- ☐ LAVATORY
- ☐ SHITTER
- ☐ LOO
- ☐ LITTLE GIRLS ROOM
- ☐ LITTLE BOYS ROOM
- ☐ COMFORT STATION
- ☐ OTHER: _____
- ☐ JOHN
- ☐ CAN
- ☐ HEAD
- ☐ POTTY
- ☐ CRAPPER
- ☐ WC

_____

RATINGS:

	1	2	3	4	5
CLEANLINESS	☆	☆	☆	☆	☆
AMBIENCE	☆	☆	☆	☆	☆
AMENITIES	☆	☆	☆	☆	☆
SOUND PROOFING	☆	☆	☆	☆	☆
QUALITY OF THE FLUSH	☆	☆	☆	☆	☆
TOILET PAPER	☆	☆	☆	☆	☆

OVERALL EXPERIENCE:

- ☐ BEST SEAT IN THE HOUSE ★★★★★
- ☐ WOULD POOP HERE AGAIN ★★★★
- ☐ SHIT GOT REAL ★★★
- ☐ SAME SHIT DIFFERENT HOUSE ★★
- ☐ THINGS JUST DIDN'T COME OUT RIGHT ★

THOUGHTS/MESSAGES: _____
_____
_____

Welcome! PLEASE SEAT YOURSELF AND ENJOY YOUR VISIT!

NAME: _____ DATE: _____ TIME: _____ DURATION OF VISIT: _____
                                                                              HRS   MIN   SEC

PURPOSE FOR VISIT: 🧻 #1 🧻 #2 🧻 OTHER: _____ SUCCESS? 🧻 YES 🧻 NO

FAVORITE EUPHEMISM FOR PERFORMING #1:

FAVORITE RESTROOM GRAFFITI OR YOUR ORIGNAL DOODLE:

FAVORITE EUPHEMISM FOR PERFORMING #2:

WHILE YOU WERE HERE, DID YOU:
- ☐ TEXT SOMEONE
- ☐ MAKE A PHONE CALL
- ☐ EMAIL
- ☐ CHECK SOCIAL MEDIA
- ☐ TAKE A SELFIE
- ☐ LOOK IN THE MEDICINE CABINET
- ☐ CHECK YOUR TEETH
- ☐ CHECK OUT YOUR BUTT
- ☐ CHECK YOUR FLY
- ☐ READ
- ☐ FIX YOUR HAIR
- ☐ TAKE SOME EXTRA "ME TIME"
- ☐ TALK TO YOURSELF
- ☐ CONDUCT BUSINESS OTHER THAN YOUR "BUSINESS." CARE TO SHARE?
  _____

FAVORITE NAME FOR THIS ROOM:
- ☐ BATHROOM
- ☐ TOILET
- ☐ POWDER ROOM
- ☐ LAVATORY
- ☐ SHITTER
- ☐ LOO
- ☐ LITTLE GIRLS ROOM
- ☐ LITTLE BOYS ROOM
- ☐ COMFORT STATION
- ☐ OTHER: _____

- ☐ JOHN
- ☐ CAN
- ☐ HEAD
- ☐ POTTY
- ☐ CRAPPER
- ☐ WC

_____

THOUGHTS/MESSAGES: _____
_____
_____

RATINGS:

	1	2	3	4	5
CLEANLINESS	☆	☆	☆	☆	☆
AMBIENCE	☆	☆	☆	☆	☆
AMENITIES	☆	☆	☆	☆	☆
SOUND PROOFING	☆	☆	☆	☆	☆
QUALITY OF THE FLUSH	☆	☆	☆	☆	☆
TOILET PAPER	☆	☆	☆	☆	☆

OVERALL EXPERIENCE:
- ☐ BEST SEAT IN THE HOUSE ★ ★ ★ ★ ★
- ☐ WOULD POOP HERE AGAIN ★ ★ ★ ★
- ☐ SHIT GOT REAL ★ ★ ★
- ☐ SAME SHIT DIFFERENT HOUSE ★ ★
- ☐ THINGS JUST DIDN'T COME OUT RIGHT ★

Welcome! PLEASE SEAT YOURSELF AND ENJOY YOUR VISIT!

NAME: _____ DATE: _____ TIME: _____ DURATION OF VISIT: _____
HRS   MIN   SEC

PURPOSE FOR VISIT: ▢ #1   ▢ #2   ▢ OTHER: _____   SUCCESS? ▢ YES ▢ NO

FAVORITE EUPHEMISM FOR PERFORMING #1: _____

FAVORITE RESTROOM GRAFFITI OR YOUR ORIGNAL DOODLE:

FAVORITE EUPHEMISM FOR PERFORMING #2: _____

WHILE YOU WERE HERE, DID YOU:
- ☐ TEXT SOMEONE
- ☐ MAKE A PHONE CALL
- ☐ EMAIL
- ☐ CHECK SOCIAL MEDIA
- ☐ TAKE A SELFIE
- ☐ LOOK IN THE MEDICINE CABINET
- ☐ CHECK YOUR TEETH
- ☐ CHECK OUT YOUR BUTT
- ☐ CHECK YOUR FLY
- ☐ READ
- ☐ FIX YOUR HAIR
- ☐ TAKE SOME EXTRA "ME TIME"
- ☐ TALK TO YOURSELF
- ☐ CONDUCT BUSINESS OTHER THAN YOUR "BUSINESS." CARE TO SHARE?

FAVORITE NAME FOR THIS ROOM:
- ☐ BATHROOM
- ☐ TOILET
- ☐ POWDER ROOM
- ☐ LAVATORY
- ☐ SHITTER
- ☐ LOO
- ☐ LITTLE GIRLS ROOM
- ☐ LITTLE BOYS ROOM
- ☐ COMFORT STATION
- ☐ OTHER: _____
- ☐ JOHN
- ☐ CAN
- ☐ HEAD
- ☐ POTTY
- ☐ CRAPPER
- ☐ WC

RATINGS:
	1	2	3	4	5
CLEANLINESS	☆	☆	☆	☆	☆
AMBIENCE	☆	☆	☆	☆	☆
AMENITIES	☆	☆	☆	☆	☆
SOUND PROOFING	☆	☆	☆	☆	☆
QUALITY OF THE FLUSH	☆	☆	☆	☆	☆
TOILET PAPER	☆	☆	☆	☆	☆

OVERALL EXPERIENCE:
- ☐ BEST SEAT IN THE HOUSE ★ ★ ★ ★ ★
- ☐ WOULD POOP HERE AGAIN ★ ★ ★ ★
- ☐ SHIT GOT REAL ★ ★ ★
- ☐ SAME SHIT DIFFERENT HOUSE ★ ★
- ☐ THINGS JUST DIDN'T COME OUT RIGHT ★

THOUGHTS/MESSAGES: _____
_____
_____

Welcome! PLEASE SEAT YOURSELF AND ENJOY YOUR VISIT!

NAME: _____ DATE: _____ TIME: _____ DURATION OF VISIT: _____
HRS   MIN   SEC

PURPOSE FOR VISIT: ▢ #1 ▢ #2 ▢ OTHER: _____ SUCCESS? ▢ YES ▢ NO

FAVORITE EUPHEMISM FOR PERFORMING #1:

FAVORITE RESTROOM GRAFFITI OR YOUR ORIGNAL DOODLE:

FAVORITE EUPHEMISM FOR PERFORMING #2:

WHILE YOU WERE HERE, DID YOU:
☐ TEXT SOMEONE
☐ MAKE A PHONE CALL
☐ EMAIL
☐ CHECK SOCIAL MEDIA
☐ TAKE A SELFIE
☐ LOOK IN THE MEDICINE CABINET
☐ CHECK YOUR TEETH
☐ CHECK OUT YOUR BUTT
☐ CHECK YOUR FLY
☐ READ
☐ FIX YOUR HAIR
☐ TAKE SOME EXTRA "ME TIME"
☐ TALK TO YOURSELF
☐ CONDUCT BUSINESS OTHER THAN YOUR "BUSINESS." CARE TO SHARE?
_____

FAVORITE NAME FOR THIS ROOM:
☐ BATHROOM
☐ TOILET
☐ POWDER ROOM
☐ LAVATORY
☐ SHITTER
☐ LOO
☐ LITTLE GIRLS ROOM
☐ LITTLE BOYS ROOM
☐ COMFORT STATION
☐ OTHER: _____

☐ JOHN
☐ CAN
☐ HEAD
☐ POTTY
☐ CRAPPER
☐ WC

RATINGS:
	1	2	3	4	5
CLEANLINESS	☆	☆	☆	☆	☆
AMBIENCE	☆	☆	☆	☆	☆
AMENITIES	☆	☆	☆	☆	☆
SOUND PROOFING	☆	☆	☆	☆	☆
QUALITY OF THE FLUSH	☆	☆	☆	☆	☆
TOILET PAPER	☆	☆	☆	☆	☆

OVERALL EXPERIENCE:
☐ BEST SEAT IN THE HOUSE ★ ★ ★ ★ ★
☐ WOULD POOP HERE AGAIN ★ ★ ★ ★
☐ SHIT GOT REAL ★ ★ ★
☐ SAME SHIT DIFFERENT HOUSE ★ ★
☐ THINGS JUST DIDN'T COME OUT RIGHT ★

THOUGHTS/MESSAGES: _____
_____
_____

Welcome! PLEASE SEAT YOURSELF AND ENJOY YOUR VISIT!

NAME: _____ DATE: _____ TIME: _____ DURATION OF VISIT: _____
HRS   MIN   SEC

PURPOSE FOR VISIT: ▢ #1 ▢ #2 ▢ OTHER: _____ SUCCESS? ▢ YES ▢ NO

FAVORITE EUPHEMISM FOR PERFORMING #1: | FAVORITE RESTROOM GRAFFITI OR YOUR ORIGNAL DOODLE:

FAVORITE EUPHEMISM FOR PERFORMING #2:

WHILE YOU WERE HERE, DID YOU:
☐ TEXT SOMEONE
☐ MAKE A PHONE CALL
☐ EMAIL
☐ CHECK SOCIAL MEDIA
☐ TAKE A SELFIE
☐ LOOK IN THE MEDICINE CABINET
☐ CHECK YOUR TEETH
☐ CHECK OUT YOUR BUTT
☐ CHECK YOUR FLY
☐ READ
☐ FIX YOUR HAIR
☐ TAKE SOME EXTRA "ME TIME"
☐ TALK TO YOURSELF
☐ CONDUCT BUSINESS OTHER THAN YOUR "BUSINESS." CARE TO SHARE?

FAVORITE NAME FOR THIS ROOM:
☐ BATHROOM   ☐ JOHN
☐ TOILET   ☐ CAN
☐ POWDER ROOM   ☐ HEAD
☐ LAVATORY   ☐ POTTY
☐ SHITTER   ☐ CRAPPER
☐ LOO   ☐ WC
☐ LITTLE GIRLS ROOM
☐ LITTLE BOYS ROOM
☐ COMFORT STATION
☐ OTHER: _____

RATINGS:
	1	2	3	4	5
CLEANLINESS	☆	☆	☆	☆	☆
AMBIENCE	☆	☆	☆	☆	☆
AMENITIES	☆	☆	☆	☆	☆
SOUND PROOFING	☆	☆	☆	☆	☆
QUALITY OF THE FLUSH	☆	☆	☆	☆	☆
TOILET PAPER	☆	☆	☆	☆	☆

OVERALL EXPERIENCE:
☐ BEST SEAT IN THE HOUSE ★ ★ ★ ★ ★
☐ WOULD POOP HERE AGAIN ★ ★ ★ ★
☐ SHIT GOT REAL ★ ★ ★
☐ SAME SHIT DIFFERENT HOUSE ★ ★
☐ THINGS JUST DIDN'T COME OUT RIGHT ★

THOUGHTS/MESSAGES: _____

Welcome! PLEASE SEAT YOURSELF AND ENJOY YOUR VISIT!

NAME: _____ DATE: _____ TIME: _____ DURATION OF VISIT: _____
                                                                    HRS   MIN   SEC

PURPOSE FOR VISIT: 🧻 #1   🧻 #2   🧻 OTHER: _____   SUCCESS? 🧻 YES 🧻 NO

FAVORITE EUPHEMISM FOR PERFORMING #1:

FAVORITE RESTROOM GRAFFITI OR YOUR ORIGNAL DOODLE:

FAVORITE EUPHEMISM FOR PERFORMING #2:

WHILE YOU WERE HERE, DID YOU:
- ☐ TEXT SOMEONE
- ☐ MAKE A PHONE CALL
- ☐ EMAIL
- ☐ CHECK SOCIAL MEDIA
- ☐ TAKE A SELFIE
- ☐ LOOK IN THE MEDICINE CABINET
- ☐ CHECK YOUR TEETH
- ☐ CHECK OUT YOUR BUTT
- ☐ CHECK YOUR FLY
- ☐ READ
- ☐ FIX YOUR HAIR
- ☐ TAKE SOME EXTRA "ME TIME"
- ☐ TALK TO YOURSELF
- ☐ CONDUCT BUSINESS OTHER THAN YOUR "BUSINESS." CARE TO SHARE?
_____

FAVORITE NAME FOR THIS ROOM:
- ☐ BATHROOM
- ☐ TOILET
- ☐ POWDER ROOM
- ☐ LAVATORY
- ☐ SHITTER
- ☐ LOO
- ☐ LITTLE GIRLS ROOM
- ☐ LITTLE BOYS ROOM
- ☐ COMFORT STATION
- ☐ OTHER: _____
- ☐ JOHN
- ☐ CAN
- ☐ HEAD
- ☐ POTTY
- ☐ CRAPPER
- ☐ WC

_____

RATINGS:
	1	2	3	4	5
CLEANLINESS	☆	☆	☆	☆	☆
AMBIENCE	☆	☆	☆	☆	☆
AMENITIES	☆	☆	☆	☆	☆
SOUND PROOFING	☆	☆	☆	☆	☆
QUALITY OF THE FLUSH	☆	☆	☆	☆	☆
TOILET PAPER	☆	☆	☆	☆	☆

OVERALL EXPERIENCE:
- ☐ BEST SEAT IN THE HOUSE ★ ★ ★ ★ ★
- ☐ WOULD POOP HERE AGAIN ★ ★ ★ ★
- ☐ SHIT GOT REAL ★ ★ ★
- ☐ SAME SHIT DIFFERENT HOUSE ★ ★
- ☐ THINGS JUST DIDN'T COME OUT RIGHT ★

THOUGHTS/MESSAGES: _____
_____
_____

Welcome! PLEASE SEAT YOURSELF AND ENJOY YOUR VISIT!

NAME: _____ DATE: _____ TIME: _____ DURATION OF VISIT: _____
HRS   MIN   SEC

PURPOSE FOR VISIT: ☐ #1 ☐ #2 ☐ OTHER: _____ SUCCESS? ☐ YES ☐ NO

FAVORITE EUPHEMISM FOR PERFORMING #1:

FAVORITE EUPHEMISM FOR PERFORMING #2:

FAVORITE RESTROOM GRAFFITI OR YOUR ORIGNAL DOODLE:

WHILE YOU WERE HERE, DID YOU:
☐ TEXT SOMEONE
☐ MAKE A PHONE CALL
☐ EMAIL
☐ CHECK SOCIAL MEDIA
☐ TAKE A SELFIE
☐ LOOK IN THE MEDICINE CABINET
☐ CHECK YOUR TEETH
☐ CHECK OUT YOUR BUTT
☐ CHECK YOUR FLY
☐ READ
☐ FIX YOUR HAIR
☐ TAKE SOME EXTRA "ME TIME"
☐ TALK TO YOURSELF
☐ CONDUCT BUSINESS OTHER THAN
YOUR "BUSINESS." CARE TO SHARE?
_____

FAVORITE NAME FOR THIS ROOM:
☐ BATHROOM   ☐ JOHN
☐ TOILET   ☐ CAN
☐ POWDER ROOM   ☐ HEAD
☐ LAVATORY   ☐ POTTY
☐ SHITTER   ☐ CRAPPER
☐ LOO   ☐ WC
☐ LITTLE GIRLS ROOM
☐ LITTLE BOYS ROOM
☐ COMFORT STATION
☐ OTHER: _____
_____

THOUGHTS/MESSAGES: _____
_____
_____

RATINGS: 1 2 3 4 5
CLEANLINESS   ☆ ☆ ☆ ☆ ☆
AMBIENCE   ☆ ☆ ☆ ☆ ☆
AMENITIES   ☆ ☆ ☆ ☆ ☆
SOUND PROOFING   ☆ ☆ ☆ ☆ ☆
QUALITY OF THE FLUSH   ☆ ☆ ☆ ☆ ☆
TOILET PAPER   ☆ ☆ ☆ ☆ ☆

OVERALL EXPERIENCE:
☐ BEST SEAT IN THE HOUSE   ★ ★ ★ ★ ★
☐ WOULD POOP HERE AGAIN   ★ ★ ★ ★
☐ SHIT GOT REAL   ★ ★ ★
☐ SAME SHIT DIFFERENT HOUSE   ★ ★
☐ THINGS JUST DIDN'T COME OUT RIGHT ★

Welcome! PLEASE SEAT YOURSELF AND ENJOY YOUR VISIT!

NAME: _____ DATE: _____ TIME: _____ DURATION OF VISIT: _____
HRS   MIN   SEC

PURPOSE FOR VISIT: ⬚ #1 ⬚ #2 ⬚ OTHER: _____ SUCCESS? ⬚ YES ⬚ NO

FAVORITE EUPHEMISM FOR PERFORMING #1:

FAVORITE RESTROOM GRAFFITI OR YOUR ORIGNAL DOODLE:

FAVORITE EUPHEMISM FOR PERFORMING #2:

WHILE YOU WERE HERE, DID YOU:
☐ TEXT SOMEONE
☐ MAKE A PHONE CALL
☐ EMAIL
☐ CHECK SOCIAL MEDIA
☐ TAKE A SELFIE
☐ LOOK IN THE MEDICINE CABINET
☐ CHECK YOUR TEETH
☐ CHECK OUT YOUR BUTT
☐ CHECK YOUR FLY
☐ READ
☐ FIX YOUR HAIR
☐ TAKE SOME EXTRA "ME TIME"
☐ TALK TO YOURSELF
☐ CONDUCT BUSINESS OTHER THAN YOUR "BUSINESS." CARE TO SHARE?
_____

FAVORITE NAME FOR THIS ROOM:
☐ BATHROOM   ☐ JOHN
☐ TOILET   ☐ CAN
☐ POWDER ROOM   ☐ HEAD
☐ LAVATORY   ☐ POTTY
☐ SHITTER   ☐ CRAPPER
☐ LOO   ☐ WC
☐ LITTLE GIRLS ROOM
☐ LITTLE BOYS ROOM
☐ COMFORT STATION
☐ OTHER: _____
_____

RATINGS:

	1	2	3	4	5
CLEANLINESS	☆	☆	☆	☆	☆
AMBIENCE	☆	☆	☆	☆	☆
AMENITIES	☆	☆	☆	☆	☆
SOUND PROOFING	☆	☆	☆	☆	☆
QUALITY OF THE FLUSH	☆	☆	☆	☆	☆
TOILET PAPER	☆	☆	☆	☆	☆

OVERALL EXPERIENCE:
☐ BEST SEAT IN THE HOUSE ★ ★ ★ ★ ★
☐ WOULD POOP HERE AGAIN ★ ★ ★ ★
☐ SHIT GOT REAL ★ ★ ★
☐ SAME SHIT DIFFERENT HOUSE ★ ★
☐ THINGS JUST DIDN'T COME OUT RIGHT ★

THOUGHTS/MESSAGES: _____
_____
_____

Welcome! PLEASE SEAT YOURSELF AND ENJOY YOUR VISIT!

NAME: _____ DATE: _____ TIME: _____ DURATION OF VISIT: _____
HRS   MIN   SEC

PURPOSE FOR VISIT: ▢ #1 ▢ #2 ▢ OTHER: _____ SUCCESS? ▢ YES ▢ NO

FAVORITE EUPHEMISM FOR PERFORMING #1:

FAVORITE RESTROOM GRAFFITI OR YOUR ORIGNAL DOODLE:

FAVORITE EUPHEMISM FOR PERFORMING #2:

WHILE YOU WERE HERE, DID YOU:
- ☐ TEXT SOMEONE
- ☐ MAKE A PHONE CALL
- ☐ EMAIL
- ☐ CHECK SOCIAL MEDIA
- ☐ TAKE A SELFIE
- ☐ LOOK IN THE MEDICINE CABINET
- ☐ CHECK YOUR TEETH
- ☐ CHECK OUT YOUR BUTT
- ☐ CHECK YOUR FLY
- ☐ READ
- ☐ FIX YOUR HAIR
- ☐ TAKE SOME EXTRA "ME TIME"
- ☐ TALK TO YOURSELF
- ☐ CONDUCT BUSINESS OTHER THAN YOUR "BUSINESS." CARE TO SHARE?

FAVORITE NAME FOR THIS ROOM:
- ☐ BATHROOM
- ☐ TOILET
- ☐ POWDER ROOM
- ☐ LAVATORY
- ☐ SHITTER
- ☐ LOO
- ☐ LITTLE GIRLS ROOM
- ☐ LITTLE BOYS ROOM
- ☐ COMFORT STATION
- ☐ OTHER: _____
- ☐ JOHN
- ☐ CAN
- ☐ HEAD
- ☐ POTTY
- ☐ CRAPPER
- ☐ WC

RATINGS:
	1	2	3	4	5
CLEANLINESS	☆	☆	☆	☆	☆
AMBIENCE	☆	☆	☆	☆	☆
AMENITIES	☆	☆	☆	☆	☆
SOUND PROOFING	☆	☆	☆	☆	☆
QUALITY OF THE FLUSH	☆	☆	☆	☆	☆
TOILET PAPER	☆	☆	☆	☆	☆

OVERALL EXPERIENCE:
- ☐ BEST SEAT IN THE HOUSE ★ ★ ★ ★ ★
- ☐ WOULD POOP HERE AGAIN ★ ★ ★ ★
- ☐ SHIT GOT REAL ★ ★ ★
- ☐ SAME SHIT DIFFERENT HOUSE ★ ★
- ☐ THINGS JUST DIDN'T COME OUT RIGHT ★

THOUGHTS/MESSAGES: _____
_____
_____

Welcome! PLEASE SEAT YOURSELF AND ENJOY YOUR VISIT!

NAME: _____ DATE: _____ TIME: _____ DURATION OF VISIT: _____
                                                                                    HRS   MIN   SEC

PURPOSE FOR VISIT: [ ] #1 [ ] #2 [ ] OTHER: _____ SUCCESS? [ ] YES [ ] NO

FAVORITE EUPHEMISM FOR PERFORMING #1:

FAVORITE RESTROOM GRAFFITI OR YOUR ORIGNAL DOODLE:

FAVORITE EUPHEMISM FOR PERFORMING #2:

WHILE YOU WERE HERE, DID YOU:
- ☐ TEXT SOMEONE
- ☐ MAKE A PHONE CALL
- ☐ EMAIL
- ☐ CHECK SOCIAL MEDIA
- ☐ TAKE A SELFIE
- ☐ LOOK IN THE MEDICINE CABINET
- ☐ CHECK YOUR TEETH
- ☐ CHECK OUT YOUR BUTT
- ☐ CHECK YOUR FLY
- ☐ READ
- ☐ FIX YOUR HAIR
- ☐ TAKE SOME EXTRA "ME TIME"
- ☐ TALK TO YOURSELF
- ☐ CONDUCT BUSINESS OTHER THAN YOUR "BUSINESS." CARE TO SHARE? _____

FAVORITE NAME FOR THIS ROOM:
- ☐ BATHROOM
- ☐ TOILET
- ☐ POWDER ROOM
- ☐ LAVATORY
- ☐ SHITTER
- ☐ LOO
- ☐ LITTLE GIRLS ROOM
- ☐ LITTLE BOYS ROOM
- ☐ COMFORT STATION
- ☐ OTHER: _____
- ☐ JOHN
- ☐ CAN
- ☐ HEAD
- ☐ POTTY
- ☐ CRAPPER
- ☐ WC

RATINGS:
	1	2	3	4	5
CLEANLINESS	☆	☆	☆	☆	☆
AMBIENCE	☆	☆	☆	☆	☆
AMENITIES	☆	☆	☆	☆	☆
SOUND PROOFING	☆	☆	☆	☆	☆
QUALITY OF THE FLUSH	☆	☆	☆	☆	☆
TOILET PAPER	☆	☆	☆	☆	☆

OVERALL EXPERIENCE:
- ☐ BEST SEAT IN THE HOUSE ★ ★ ★ ★ ★
- ☐ WOULD POOP HERE AGAIN ★ ★ ★ ★
- ☐ SHIT GOT REAL ★ ★ ★
- ☐ SAME SHIT DIFFERENT HOUSE ★ ★
- ☐ THINGS JUST DIDN'T COME OUT RIGHT ★

THOUGHTS/MESSAGES: _____
_____
_____

Welcome! PLEASE SEAT YOURSELF AND ENJOY YOUR VISIT!

NAME: _____ DATE: _____ TIME: _____ DURATION OF VISIT: _____

HRS   MIN   SEC

PURPOSE FOR VISIT: ☐ #1   ☐ #2   ☐ OTHER: _____   SUCCESS? ☐ YES ☐ NO

FAVORITE EUPHEMISM FOR PERFORMING #1:

FAVORITE RESTROOM GRAFFITI OR YOUR ORIGNAL DOODLE:

FAVORITE EUPHEMISM FOR PERFORMING #2:

WHILE YOU WERE HERE, DID YOU:
☐ TEXT SOMEONE
☐ MAKE A PHONE CALL
☐ EMAIL
☐ CHECK SOCIAL MEDIA
☐ TAKE A SELFIE
☐ LOOK IN THE MEDICINE CABINET
☐ CHECK YOUR TEETH
☐ CHECK OUT YOUR BUTT
☐ CHECK YOUR FLY
☐ READ
☐ FIX YOUR HAIR
☐ TAKE SOME EXTRA "ME TIME"
☐ TALK TO YOURSELF
☐ CONDUCT BUSINESS OTHER THAN YOUR "BUSINESS." CARE TO SHARE?

FAVORITE NAME FOR THIS ROOM:
☐ BATHROOM   ☐ JOHN
☐ TOILET   ☐ CAN
☐ POWDER ROOM   ☐ HEAD
☐ LAVATORY   ☐ POTTY
☐ SHITTER   ☐ CRAPPER
☐ LOO   ☐ WC
☐ LITTLE GIRLS ROOM
☐ LITTLE BOYS ROOM
☐ COMFORT STATION
☐ OTHER: _____

RATINGS:
	1	2	3	4	5
CLEANLINESS	☆	☆	☆	☆	☆
AMBIENCE	☆	☆	☆	☆	☆
AMENITIES	☆	☆	☆	☆	☆
SOUND PROOFING	☆	☆	☆	☆	☆
QUALITY OF THE FLUSH	☆	☆	☆	☆	☆
TOILET PAPER	☆	☆	☆	☆	☆

OVERALL EXPERIENCE:
☐ BEST SEAT IN THE HOUSE ★ ★ ★ ★ ★
☐ WOULD POOP HERE AGAIN ★ ★ ★ ★
☐ SHIT GOT REAL ★ ★ ★
☐ SAME SHIT DIFFERENT HOUSE ★ ★
☐ THINGS JUST DIDN'T COME OUT RIGHT ★

THOUGHTS/MESSAGES: _____

Welcome! PLEASE SEAT YOURSELF AND ENJOY YOUR VISIT!

NAME: _____ DATE: _____ TIME: _____ DURATION OF VISIT: _____
HRS   MIN   SEC

PURPOSE FOR VISIT: 🧻 #1   🧻 #2   🧻 OTHER: _____   SUCCESS? 🧻 YES 🧻 NO

FAVORITE EUPHEMISM FOR PERFORMING #1:

FAVORITE RESTROOM GRAFFITI OR YOUR ORIGNAL DOODLE:

FAVORITE EUPHEMISM FOR PERFORMING #2:

WHILE YOU WERE HERE, DID YOU:
- ☐ TEXT SOMEONE
- ☐ MAKE A PHONE CALL
- ☐ EMAIL
- ☐ CHECK SOCIAL MEDIA
- ☐ TAKE A SELFIE
- ☐ LOOK IN THE MEDICINE CABINET
- ☐ CHECK YOUR TEETH
- ☐ CHECK OUT YOUR BUTT
- ☐ CHECK YOUR FLY
- ☐ READ
- ☐ FIX YOUR HAIR
- ☐ TAKE SOME EXTRA "ME TIME"
- ☐ TALK TO YOURSELF
- ☐ CONDUCT BUSINESS OTHER THAN YOUR "BUSINESS." CARE TO SHARE?
_____

FAVORITE NAME FOR THIS ROOM:
- ☐ BATHROOM
- ☐ TOILET
- ☐ POWDER ROOM
- ☐ LAVATORY
- ☐ SHITTER
- ☐ LOO
- ☐ LITTLE GIRLS ROOM
- ☐ LITTLE BOYS ROOM
- ☐ COMFORT STATION
- ☐ OTHER: _____
- ☐ JOHN
- ☐ CAN
- ☐ HEAD
- ☐ POTTY
- ☐ CRAPPER
- ☐ WC

_____

THOUGHTS/MESSAGES: _____
_____
_____

RATINGS: 1 2 3 4 5
CLEANLINESS   ☆ ☆ ☆ ☆ ☆
AMBIENCE   ☆ ☆ ☆ ☆ ☆
AMENITIES   ☆ ☆ ☆ ☆ ☆
SOUND PROOFING   ☆ ☆ ☆ ☆ ☆
QUALITY OF THE FLUSH ☆ ☆ ☆ ☆ ☆
TOILET PAPER   ☆ ☆ ☆ ☆ ☆

OVERALL EXPERIENCE:
- ☐ BEST SEAT IN THE HOUSE   ★ ★ ★ ★ ★
- ☐ WOULD POOP HERE AGAIN   ★ ★ ★ ★
- ☐ SHIT GOT REAL   ★ ★ ★
- ☐ SAME SHIT DIFFERENT HOUSE   ★ ★
- ☐ THINGS JUST DIDN'T COME OUT RIGHT ★

Welcome! PLEASE SEAT YOURSELF AND ENJOY YOUR VISIT!

NAME: _____ DATE: _____ TIME: _____ DURATION OF VISIT: _____
HRS   MIN   SEC

PURPOSE FOR VISIT: 🧻 #1 🧻 #2 🧻 OTHER: _____ SUCCESS? 🧻 YES 🧻 NO

FAVORITE EUPHEMISM FOR PERFORMING #1: | **FAVORITE RESTROOM GRAFFITI OR YOUR ORIGNAL DOODLE:**

FAVORITE EUPHEMISM FOR PERFORMING #2:

WHILE YOU WERE HERE, DID YOU:
- ☐ TEXT SOMEONE
- ☐ MAKE A PHONE CALL
- ☐ EMAIL
- ☐ CHECK SOCIAL MEDIA
- ☐ TAKE A SELFIE
- ☐ LOOK IN THE MEDICINE CABINET
- ☐ CHECK YOUR TEETH
- ☐ CHECK OUT YOUR BUTT
- ☐ CHECK YOUR FLY
- ☐ READ
- ☐ FIX YOUR HAIR
- ☐ TAKE SOME EXTRA "ME TIME"
- ☐ TALK TO YOURSELF
- ☐ CONDUCT BUSINESS OTHER THAN YOUR "BUSINESS." CARE TO SHARE?

FAVORITE NAME FOR THIS ROOM:
- ☐ BATHROOM
- ☐ TOILET
- ☐ POWDER ROOM
- ☐ LAVATORY
- ☐ SHITTER
- ☐ LOO
- ☐ LITTLE GIRLS ROOM
- ☐ LITTLE BOYS ROOM
- ☐ COMFORT STATION
- ☐ OTHER: _____
- ☐ JOHN
- ☐ CAN
- ☐ HEAD
- ☐ POTTY
- ☐ CRAPPER
- ☐ WC

RATINGS:
	1	2	3	4	5
CLEANLINESS	☆	☆	☆	☆	☆
AMBIENCE	☆	☆	☆	☆	☆
AMENITIES	☆	☆	☆	☆	☆
SOUND PROOFING	☆	☆	☆	☆	☆
QUALITY OF THE FLUSH	☆	☆	☆	☆	☆
TOILET PAPER	☆	☆	☆	☆	☆

OVERALL EXPERIENCE:
- ☐ BEST SEAT IN THE HOUSE ★ ★ ★ ★ ★
- ☐ WOULD POOP HERE AGAIN ★ ★ ★ ★
- ☐ SHIT GOT REAL ★ ★ ★
- ☐ SAME SHIT DIFFERENT HOUSE ★ ★
- ☐ THINGS JUST DIDN'T COME OUT RIGHT ★

THOUGHTS/MESSAGES: _____
_____
_____

Welcome! PLEASE SEAT YOURSELF AND ENJOY YOUR VISIT!

NAME: _____ DATE: _____ TIME: _____ DURATION OF VISIT: _____

HRS   MIN   SEC

PURPOSE FOR VISIT: 🧻 #1   🧻 #2   🧻 OTHER: _____   SUCCESS? 🧻 YES   🧻 NO

FAVORITE EUPHEMISM FOR PERFORMING #1:

FAVORITE RESTROOM GRAFFITI OR YOUR ORIGNAL DOODLE:

FAVORITE EUPHEMISM FOR PERFORMING #2:

WHILE YOU WERE HERE, DID YOU:

☐ TEXT SOMEONE
☐ MAKE A PHONE CALL
☐ EMAIL
☐ CHECK SOCIAL MEDIA
☐ TAKE A SELFIE
☐ LOOK IN THE MEDICINE CABINET
☐ CHECK YOUR TEETH
☐ CHECK OUT YOUR BUTT
☐ CHECK YOUR FLY
☐ READ
☐ FIX YOUR HAIR
☐ TAKE SOME EXTRA "ME TIME"
☐ TALK TO YOURSELF
☐ CONDUCT BUSINESS OTHER THAN YOUR "BUSINESS." CARE TO SHARE?
_____

FAVORITE NAME FOR THIS ROOM:

☐ BATHROOM
☐ TOILET
☐ POWDER ROOM
☐ LAVATORY
☐ SHITTER
☐ LOO
☐ LITTLE GIRLS ROOM
☐ LITTLE BOYS ROOM
☐ COMFORT STATION
☐ OTHER: _____

☐ JOHN
☐ CAN
☐ HEAD
☐ POTTY
☐ CRAPPER
☐ WC

_____
_____

THOUGHTS/MESSAGES: _____
_____
_____

RATINGS:

	1	2	3	4	5
CLEANLINESS	☆	☆	☆	☆	☆
AMBIENCE	☆	☆	☆	☆	☆
AMENITIES	☆	☆	☆	☆	☆
SOUND PROOFING	☆	☆	☆	☆	☆
QUALITY OF THE FLUSH	☆	☆	☆	☆	☆
TOILET PAPER	☆	☆	☆	☆	☆

OVERALL EXPERIENCE:

☐ BEST SEAT IN THE HOUSE ★ ★ ★ ★ ★
☐ WOULD POOP HERE AGAIN ★ ★ ★ ★
☐ SHIT GOT REAL ★ ★ ★
☐ SAME SHIT DIFFERENT HOUSE ★ ★
☐ THINGS JUST DIDN'T COME OUT RIGHT ★

Welcome! PLEASE SEAT YOURSELF AND ENJOY YOUR VISIT!

NAME: _____ DATE: _____ TIME: _____ DURATION OF VISIT: _____

HRS   MIN   SEC

PURPOSE FOR VISIT: ▢ #1 ▢ #2 ▢ OTHER: _____ SUCCESS? ▢ YES ▢ NO

FAVORITE EUPHEMISM FOR PERFORMING #1:

FAVORITE RESTROOM GRAFFITI OR YOUR ORIGNAL DOODLE:

FAVORITE EUPHEMISM FOR PERFORMING #2:

WHILE YOU WERE HERE, DID YOU:
- ☐ TEXT SOMEONE
- ☐ MAKE A PHONE CALL
- ☐ EMAIL
- ☐ CHECK SOCIAL MEDIA
- ☐ TAKE A SELFIE
- ☐ LOOK IN THE MEDICINE CABINET
- ☐ CHECK YOUR TEETH
- ☐ CHECK OUT YOUR BUTT
- ☐ CHECK YOUR FLY
- ☐ READ
- ☐ FIX YOUR HAIR
- ☐ TAKE SOME EXTRA "ME TIME"
- ☐ TALK TO YOURSELF
- ☐ CONDUCT BUSINESS OTHER THAN YOUR "BUSINESS." CARE TO SHARE?
_____

FAVORITE NAME FOR THIS ROOM:
- ☐ BATHROOM
- ☐ TOILET
- ☐ POWDER ROOM
- ☐ LAVATORY
- ☐ SHITTER
- ☐ LOO
- ☐ LITTLE GIRLS ROOM
- ☐ LITTLE BOYS ROOM
- ☐ COMFORT STATION
- ☐ OTHER: _____
- ☐ JOHN
- ☐ CAN
- ☐ HEAD
- ☐ POTTY
- ☐ CRAPPER
- ☐ WC

_____

THOUGHTS/MESSAGES: _____
_____
_____

RATINGS:
	1	2	3	4	5
CLEANLINESS	☆	☆	☆	☆	☆
AMBIENCE	☆	☆	☆	☆	☆
AMENITIES	☆	☆	☆	☆	☆
SOUND PROOFING	☆	☆	☆	☆	☆
QUALITY OF THE FLUSH	☆	☆	☆	☆	☆
TOILET PAPER	☆	☆	☆	☆	☆

OVERALL EXPERIENCE:
- ☐ BEST SEAT IN THE HOUSE ★ ★ ★ ★ ★
- ☐ WOULD POOP HERE AGAIN ★ ★ ★ ★
- ☐ SHIT GOT REAL ★ ★ ★
- ☐ SAME SHIT DIFFERENT HOUSE ★ ★
- ☐ THINGS JUST DIDN'T COME OUT RIGHT ★

Welcome! PLEASE SEAT YOURSELF AND ENJOY YOUR VISIT!

NAME: _____ DATE: _____ TIME: _____ DURATION OF VISIT: _____
HRS   MIN   SEC

PURPOSE FOR VISIT: 🧻 #1   🧻 #2   🧻 OTHER: _____   SUCCESS? 🧻 YES   🧻 NO

FAVORITE EUPHEMISM FOR PERFORMING #1:

FAVORITE RESTROOM GRAFFITI OR YOUR ORIGNAL DOODLE:

FAVORITE EUPHEMISM FOR PERFORMING #2:

WHILE YOU WERE HERE, DID YOU:
- ☐ TEXT SOMEONE
- ☐ MAKE A PHONE CALL
- ☐ EMAIL
- ☐ CHECK SOCIAL MEDIA
- ☐ TAKE A SELFIE
- ☐ LOOK IN THE MEDICINE CABINET
- ☐ CHECK YOUR TEETH
- ☐ CHECK OUT YOUR BUTT
- ☐ CHECK YOUR FLY
- ☐ READ
- ☐ FIX YOUR HAIR
- ☐ TAKE SOME EXTRA "ME TIME"
- ☐ TALK TO YOURSELF
- ☐ CONDUCT BUSINESS OTHER THAN YOUR "BUSINESS." CARE TO SHARE?

FAVORITE NAME FOR THIS ROOM:
- ☐ BATHROOM
- ☐ TOILET
- ☐ POWDER ROOM
- ☐ LAVATORY
- ☐ SHITTER
- ☐ LOO
- ☐ LITTLE GIRLS ROOM
- ☐ LITTLE BOYS ROOM
- ☐ COMFORT STATION
- ☐ OTHER: _____
- ☐ JOHN
- ☐ CAN
- ☐ HEAD
- ☐ POTTY
- ☐ CRAPPER
- ☐ WC

RATINGS:

	1	2	3	4	5
CLEANLINESS	☆	☆	☆	☆	☆
AMBIENCE	☆	☆	☆	☆	☆
AMENITIES	☆	☆	☆	☆	☆
SOUND PROOFING	☆	☆	☆	☆	☆
QUALITY OF THE FLUSH	☆	☆	☆	☆	☆
TOILET PAPER	☆	☆	☆	☆	☆

OVERALL EXPERIENCE:
- ☐ BEST SEAT IN THE HOUSE ★ ★ ★ ★ ★
- ☐ WOULD POOP HERE AGAIN ★ ★ ★ ★
- ☐ SHIT GOT REAL ★ ★ ★
- ☐ SAME SHIT DIFFERENT HOUSE ★ ★
- ☐ THINGS JUST DIDN'T COME OUT RIGHT ★

THOUGHTS/MESSAGES: _____
_____
_____

Welcome! PLEASE SEAT YOURSELF AND ENJOY YOUR VISIT!

NAME: _____ DATE: _____ TIME: _____ DURATION OF VISIT: _____
HRS   MIN   SEC

PURPOSE FOR VISIT: ☐ #1   ☐ #2   ☐ OTHER: _____   SUCCESS? ☐ YES ☐ NO

FAVORITE EUPHEMISM FOR PERFORMING #1:

FAVORITE EUPHEMISM FOR PERFORMING #2:

FAVORITE RESTROOM GRAFFITI OR YOUR ORIGNAL DOODLE:

WHILE YOU WERE HERE, DID YOU:
☐ TEXT SOMEONE
☐ MAKE A PHONE CALL
☐ EMAIL
☐ CHECK SOCIAL MEDIA
☐ TAKE A SELFIE
☐ LOOK IN THE MEDICINE CABINET
☐ CHECK YOUR TEETH
☐ CHECK OUT YOUR BUTT
☐ CHECK YOUR FLY
☐ READ
☐ FIX YOUR HAIR
☐ TAKE SOME EXTRA "ME TIME"
☐ TALK TO YOURSELF
☐ CONDUCT BUSINESS OTHER THAN YOUR "BUSINESS." CARE TO SHARE?

FAVORITE NAME FOR THIS ROOM:
☐ BATHROOM   ☐ JOHN
☐ TOILET   ☐ CAN
☐ POWDER ROOM   ☐ HEAD
☐ LAVATORY   ☐ POTTY
☐ SHITTER   ☐ CRAPPER
☐ LOO   ☐ WC
☐ LITTLE GIRLS ROOM
☐ LITTLE BOYS ROOM
☐ COMFORT STATION
☐ OTHER: _____

THOUGHTS/MESSAGES: _____

RATINGS: 1 2 3 4 5
CLEANLINESS   ☆ ☆ ☆ ☆ ☆
AMBIENCE   ☆ ☆ ☆ ☆ ☆
AMENITIES   ☆ ☆ ☆ ☆ ☆
SOUND PROOFING   ☆ ☆ ☆ ☆ ☆
QUALITY OF THE FLUSH   ☆ ☆ ☆ ☆ ☆
TOILET PAPER   ☆ ☆ ☆ ☆ ☆

OVERALL EXPERIENCE:
☐ BEST SEAT IN THE HOUSE   ★ ★ ★ ★ ★
☐ WOULD POOP HERE AGAIN   ★ ★ ★ ★
☐ SHIT GOT REAL   ★ ★ ★
☐ SAME SHIT DIFFERENT HOUSE   ★ ★
☐ THINGS JUST DIDN'T COME OUT RIGHT   ★

Welcome! PLEASE SEAT YOURSELF AND ENJOY YOUR VISIT!

NAME: _____ DATE: _____ TIME: _____ DURATION OF VISIT: _____
HRS   MIN   SEC

PURPOSE FOR VISIT: ☐ #1 ☐ #2 ☐ OTHER: _____ SUCCESS? ☐ YES ☐ NO

FAVORITE EUPHEMISM FOR PERFORMING #1:

FAVORITE RESTROOM GRAFFITI OR YOUR ORIGNAL DOODLE:

FAVORITE EUPHEMISM FOR PERFORMING #2:

WHILE YOU WERE HERE, DID YOU:
☐ TEXT SOMEONE
☐ MAKE A PHONE CALL
☐ EMAIL
☐ CHECK SOCIAL MEDIA
☐ TAKE A SELFIE
☐ LOOK IN THE MEDICINE CABINET
☐ CHECK YOUR TEETH
☐ CHECK OUT YOUR BUTT
☐ CHECK YOUR FLY
☐ READ
☐ FIX YOUR HAIR
☐ TAKE SOME EXTRA "ME TIME"
☐ TALK TO YOURSELF
☐ CONDUCT BUSINESS OTHER THAN YOUR "BUSINESS." CARE TO SHARE?
_____

FAVORITE NAME FOR THIS ROOM:
☐ BATHROOM   ☐ JOHN
☐ TOILET   ☐ CAN
☐ POWDER ROOM   ☐ HEAD
☐ LAVATORY   ☐ POTTY
☐ SHITTER   ☐ CRAPPER
☐ LOO   ☐ WC
☐ LITTLE GIRLS ROOM
☐ LITTLE BOYS ROOM
☐ COMFORT STATION
☐ OTHER: _____

RATINGS: 1 2 3 4 5
CLEANLINESS   ☆ ☆ ☆ ☆ ☆
AMBIENCE   ☆ ☆ ☆ ☆ ☆
AMENITIES   ☆ ☆ ☆ ☆ ☆
SOUND PROOFING   ☆ ☆ ☆ ☆ ☆
QUALITY OF THE FLUSH   ☆ ☆ ☆ ☆ ☆
TOILET PAPER   ☆ ☆ ☆ ☆ ☆

OVERALL EXPERIENCE:
☐ BEST SEAT IN THE HOUSE   ★ ★ ★ ★ ★
☐ WOULD POOP HERE AGAIN   ★ ★ ★ ★
☐ SHIT GOT REAL   ★ ★ ★
☐ SAME SHIT DIFFERENT HOUSE   ★ ★
☐ THINGS JUST DIDN'T COME OUT RIGHT ★

THOUGHTS/MESSAGES: _____
_____
_____

Welcome! PLEASE SEAT YOURSELF AND ENJOY YOUR VISIT!

NAME: _____ DATE: _____ TIME: _____ DURATION OF VISIT: _____

HRS   MIN   SEC

PURPOSE FOR VISIT: ▢ #1 ▢ #2 ▢ OTHER: _____ SUCCESS? ▢ YES ▢ NO

FAVORITE EUPHEMISM FOR PERFORMING #1: | FAVORITE RESTROOM GRAFFITI OR YOUR ORIGNAL DOODLE:

FAVORITE EUPHEMISM FOR PERFORMING #2:

WHILE YOU WERE HERE, DID YOU:
- ☐ TEXT SOMEONE
- ☐ MAKE A PHONE CALL
- ☐ EMAIL
- ☐ CHECK SOCIAL MEDIA
- ☐ TAKE A SELFIE
- ☐ LOOK IN THE MEDICINE CABINET
- ☐ CHECK YOUR TEETH
- ☐ CHECK OUT YOUR BUTT
- ☐ CHECK YOUR FLY
- ☐ READ
- ☐ FIX YOUR HAIR
- ☐ TAKE SOME EXTRA "ME TIME"
- ☐ TALK TO YOURSELF
- ☐ CONDUCT BUSINESS OTHER THAN YOUR "BUSINESS." CARE TO SHARE?

FAVORITE NAME FOR THIS ROOM:
- ☐ BATHROOM
- ☐ TOILET
- ☐ POWDER ROOM
- ☐ LAVATORY
- ☐ SHITTER
- ☐ LOO
- ☐ LITTLE GIRLS ROOM
- ☐ LITTLE BOYS ROOM
- ☐ COMFORT STATION
- ☐ OTHER: _____
- ☐ JOHN
- ☐ CAN
- ☐ HEAD
- ☐ POTTY
- ☐ CRAPPER
- ☐ WC

RATINGS:
	1 2 3 4 5
CLEANLINESS	☆ ☆ ☆ ☆ ☆
AMBIENCE	☆ ☆ ☆ ☆ ☆
AMENITIES	☆ ☆ ☆ ☆ ☆
SOUND PROOFING	☆ ☆ ☆ ☆ ☆
QUALITY OF THE FLUSH	☆ ☆ ☆ ☆ ☆
TOILET PAPER	☆ ☆ ☆ ☆ ☆

OVERALL EXPERIENCE:
- ☐ BEST SEAT IN THE HOUSE ★ ★ ★ ★ ★
- ☐ WOULD POOP HERE AGAIN ★ ★ ★ ★
- ☐ SHIT GOT REAL ★ ★ ★
- ☐ SAME SHIT DIFFERENT HOUSE ★ ★
- ☐ THINGS JUST DIDN'T COME OUT RIGHT ★

THOUGHTS/MESSAGES: _____

Welcome! PLEASE SEAT YOURSELF AND ENJOY YOUR VISIT!

NAME: _____ DATE: _____ TIME: _____ DURATION OF VISIT: _____

HRS   MIN   SEC

PURPOSE FOR VISIT: ☐ #1   ☐ #2   ☐ OTHER: _____   SUCCESS? ☐ YES ☐ NO

FAVORITE EUPHEMISM FOR PERFORMING #1:

FAVORITE RESTROOM GRAFFITI OR YOUR ORIGNAL DOODLE:

FAVORITE EUPHEMISM FOR PERFORMING #2:

WHILE YOU WERE HERE, DID YOU:

☐ TEXT SOMEONE
☐ MAKE A PHONE CALL
☐ EMAIL
☐ CHECK SOCIAL MEDIA
☐ TAKE A SELFIE
☐ LOOK IN THE MEDICINE CABINET
☐ CHECK YOUR TEETH
☐ CHECK OUT YOUR BUTT
☐ CHECK YOUR FLY
☐ READ
☐ FIX YOUR HAIR
☐ TAKE SOME EXTRA "ME TIME"
☐ TALK TO YOURSELF
☐ CONDUCT BUSINESS OTHER THAN YOUR "BUSINESS." CARE TO SHARE?
_____

FAVORITE NAME FOR THIS ROOM:

☐ BATHROOM
☐ TOILET
☐ POWDER ROOM
☐ LAVATORY
☐ SHITTER
☐ LOO
☐ LITTLE GIRLS ROOM
☐ LITTLE BOYS ROOM
☐ COMFORT STATION
☐ OTHER: _____
_____

☐ JOHN
☐ CAN
☐ HEAD
☐ POTTY
☐ CRAPPER
☐ WC

RATINGS:

	1	2	3	4	5
CLEANLINESS	☆	☆	☆	☆	☆
AMBIENCE	☆	☆	☆	☆	☆
AMENITIES	☆	☆	☆	☆	☆
SOUND PROOFING	☆	☆	☆	☆	☆
QUALITY OF THE FLUSH	☆	☆	☆	☆	☆
TOILET PAPER	☆	☆	☆	☆	☆

OVERALL EXPERIENCE:

☐ BEST SEAT IN THE HOUSE   ★ ★ ★ ★ ★
☐ WOULD POOP HERE AGAIN   ★ ★ ★ ★
☐ SHIT GOT REAL   ★ ★ ★
☐ SAME SHIT DIFFERENT HOUSE   ★ ★
☐ THINGS JUST DIDN'T COME OUT RIGHT   ★

THOUGHTS/MESSAGES: _____
_____
_____

Welcome! PLEASE SEAT YOURSELF AND ENJOY YOUR VISIT!

NAME: _____ **DATE:** _____ **TIME:** _____ **DURATION OF VISIT:** _____
HRS   MIN   SEC

PURPOSE FOR VISIT: ▢ #1 ▢ #2 ▢ **OTHER:** _____ **SUCCESS?** ▢ YES ▢ NO

FAVORITE EUPHEMISM FOR PERFORMING #1: _____

FAVORITE RESTROOM GRAFFITI OR YOUR ORIGNAL DOODLE:

FAVORITE EUPHEMISM FOR PERFORMING #2: _____

WHILE YOU WERE HERE, DID YOU:
- ▢ TEXT SOMEONE
- ▢ MAKE A PHONE CALL
- ▢ EMAIL
- ▢ CHECK SOCIAL MEDIA
- ▢ TAKE A SELFIE
- ▢ LOOK IN THE MEDICINE CABINET
- ▢ CHECK YOUR TEETH
- ▢ CHECK OUT YOUR BUTT
- ▢ CHECK YOUR FLY
- ▢ READ
- ▢ FIX YOUR HAIR
- ▢ TAKE SOME EXTRA "ME TIME"
- ▢ TALK TO YOURSELF
- ▢ CONDUCT BUSINESS OTHER THAN YOUR "BUSINESS." CARE TO SHARE?
  _____

FAVORITE NAME FOR THIS ROOM:
- ▢ BATHROOM
- ▢ TOILET
- ▢ POWDER ROOM
- ▢ LAVATORY
- ▢ SHITTER
- ▢ LOO
- ▢ LITTLE GIRLS ROOM
- ▢ LITTLE BOYS ROOM
- ▢ COMFORT STATION
- ▢ OTHER: _____
- ▢ JOHN
- ▢ CAN
- ▢ HEAD
- ▢ POTTY
- ▢ CRAPPER
- ▢ WC

RATINGS:
	1	2	3	4	5
CLEANLINESS	☆	☆	☆	☆	☆
AMBIENCE	☆	☆	☆	☆	☆
AMENITIES	☆	☆	☆	☆	☆
SOUND PROOFING	☆	☆	☆	☆	☆
QUALITY OF THE FLUSH	☆	☆	☆	☆	☆
TOILET PAPER	☆	☆	☆	☆	☆

OVERALL EXPERIENCE:
- ▢ BEST SEAT IN THE HOUSE ★ ★ ★ ★ ★
- ▢ WOULD POOP HERE AGAIN ★ ★ ★ ★
- ▢ SHIT GOT REAL ★ ★ ★
- ▢ SAME SHIT DIFFERENT HOUSE ★ ★
- ▢ THINGS JUST DIDN'T COME OUT RIGHT ★

THOUGHTS/MESSAGES: _____

Welcome! PLEASE SEAT YOURSELF AND ENJOY YOUR VISIT!

NAME: _____ DATE: _____ TIME: _____ DURATION OF VISIT: _____
HRS   MIN   SEC

PURPOSE FOR VISIT: [ ] #1 [ ] #2 [ ] OTHER: _____   SUCCESS? [ ] YES [ ] NO

FAVORITE EUPHEMISM FOR PERFORMING #1:

FAVORITE RESTROOM GRAFFITI OR YOUR ORIGNAL DOODLE:

FAVORITE EUPHEMISM FOR PERFORMING #2:

WHILE YOU WERE HERE, DID YOU:
- ☐ TEXT SOMEONE
- ☐ MAKE A PHONE CALL
- ☐ EMAIL
- ☐ CHECK SOCIAL MEDIA
- ☐ TAKE A SELFIE
- ☐ LOOK IN THE MEDICINE CABINET
- ☐ CHECK YOUR TEETH
- ☐ CHECK OUT YOUR BUTT
- ☐ CHECK YOUR FLY
- ☐ READ
- ☐ FIX YOUR HAIR
- ☐ TAKE SOME EXTRA "ME TIME"
- ☐ TALK TO YOURSELF
- ☐ CONDUCT BUSINESS OTHER THAN YOUR "BUSINESS." CARE TO SHARE?
  _____

FAVORITE NAME FOR THIS ROOM:
- ☐ BATHROOM
- ☐ TOILET
- ☐ POWDER ROOM
- ☐ LAVATORY
- ☐ SHITTER
- ☐ LOO
- ☐ LITTLE GIRLS ROOM
- ☐ LITTLE BOYS ROOM
- ☐ COMFORT STATION
- ☐ OTHER: _____

- ☐ JOHN
- ☐ CAN
- ☐ HEAD
- ☐ POTTY
- ☐ CRAPPER
- ☐ WC

RATINGS:
	1	2	3	4	5
CLEANLINESS	☆	☆	☆	☆	☆
AMBIENCE	☆	☆	☆	☆	☆
AMENITIES	☆	☆	☆	☆	☆
SOUND PROOFING	☆	☆	☆	☆	☆
QUALITY OF THE FLUSH	☆	☆	☆	☆	☆
TOILET PAPER	☆	☆	☆	☆	☆

OVERALL EXPERIENCE:
- ☐ BEST SEAT IN THE HOUSE ★ ★ ★ ★ ★
- ☐ WOULD POOP HERE AGAIN ★ ★ ★ ★
- ☐ SHIT GOT REAL ★ ★ ★
- ☐ SAME SHIT DIFFERENT HOUSE ★ ★
- ☐ THINGS JUST DIDN'T COME OUT RIGHT ★

THOUGHTS/MESSAGES: _____
_____
_____

Welcome! PLEASE SEAT YOURSELF AND ENJOY YOUR VISIT!

NAME: _____ DATE: _____ TIME: _____ DURATION OF VISIT: _____
HRS   MIN   SEC

PURPOSE FOR VISIT: 🧻 #1 🧻 #2 🧻 OTHER: _____ SUCCESS? 🧻 YES 🧻 NO

FAVORITE EUPHEMISM FOR PERFORMING #1:

FAVORITE EUPHEMISM FOR PERFORMING #2:

FAVORITE RESTROOM GRAFFITI OR YOUR ORIGNAL DOODLE:

WHILE YOU WERE HERE, DID YOU:
- ☐ TEXT SOMEONE
- ☐ MAKE A PHONE CALL
- ☐ EMAIL
- ☐ CHECK SOCIAL MEDIA
- ☐ TAKE A SELFIE
- ☐ LOOK IN THE MEDICINE CABINET
- ☐ CHECK YOUR TEETH
- ☐ CHECK OUT YOUR BUTT
- ☐ CHECK YOUR FLY
- ☐ READ
- ☐ FIX YOUR HAIR
- ☐ TAKE SOME EXTRA "ME TIME"
- ☐ TALK TO YOURSELF
- ☐ CONDUCT BUSINESS OTHER THAN YOUR "BUSINESS." CARE TO SHARE?
  _____

FAVORITE NAME FOR THIS ROOM:
- ☐ BATHROOM
- ☐ TOILET
- ☐ POWDER ROOM
- ☐ LAVATORY
- ☐ SHITTER
- ☐ LOO
- ☐ LITTLE GIRLS ROOM
- ☐ LITTLE BOYS ROOM
- ☐ COMFORT STATION
- ☐ OTHER: _____
- ☐ JOHN
- ☐ CAN
- ☐ HEAD
- ☐ POTTY
- ☐ CRAPPER
- ☐ WC

THOUGHTS/MESSAGES: _____

RATINGS:
	1 2 3 4 5
CLEANLINESS	☆ ☆ ☆ ☆ ☆
AMBIENCE	☆ ☆ ☆ ☆ ☆
AMENITIES	☆ ☆ ☆ ☆ ☆
SOUND PROOFING	☆ ☆ ☆ ☆ ☆
QUALITY OF THE FLUSH	☆ ☆ ☆ ☆ ☆
TOILET PAPER	☆ ☆ ☆ ☆ ☆

OVERALL EXPERIENCE:
- ☐ BEST SEAT IN THE HOUSE ★ ★ ★ ★ ★
- ☐ WOULD POOP HERE AGAIN ★ ★ ★ ★
- ☐ SHIT GOT REAL ★ ★ ★
- ☐ SAME SHIT DIFFERENT HOUSE ★ ★
- ☐ THINGS JUST DIDN'T COME OUT RIGHT ★

Welcome! PLEASE SEAT YOURSELF AND ENJOY YOUR VISIT!

NAME: _____ DATE: _____ TIME: _____ DURATION OF VISIT: _____
HRS   MIN   SEC

PURPOSE FOR VISIT: 🧻 #1 🧻 #2 🧻 OTHER: _____ SUCCESS? 🧻 YES 🧻 NO

FAVORITE EUPHEMISM FOR PERFORMING #1:

FAVORITE RESTROOM GRAFFITI OR YOUR ORIGNAL DOODLE:

FAVORITE EUPHEMISM FOR PERFORMING #2:

WHILE YOU WERE HERE, DID YOU:
- ☐ TEXT SOMEONE
- ☐ MAKE A PHONE CALL
- ☐ EMAIL
- ☐ CHECK SOCIAL MEDIA
- ☐ TAKE A SELFIE
- ☐ LOOK IN THE MEDICINE CABINET
- ☐ CHECK YOUR TEETH
- ☐ CHECK OUT YOUR BUTT
- ☐ CHECK YOUR FLY
- ☐ READ
- ☐ FIX YOUR HAIR
- ☐ TAKE SOME EXTRA "ME TIME"
- ☐ TALK TO YOURSELF
- ☐ CONDUCT BUSINESS OTHER THAN YOUR "BUSINESS." CARE TO SHARE?
_____

FAVORITE NAME FOR THIS ROOM:
- ☐ BATHROOM
- ☐ TOILET
- ☐ POWDER ROOM
- ☐ LAVATORY
- ☐ SHITTER
- ☐ LOO
- ☐ LITTLE GIRLS ROOM
- ☐ LITTLE BOYS ROOM
- ☐ COMFORT STATION
- ☐ OTHER: _____
- ☐ JOHN
- ☐ CAN
- ☐ HEAD
- ☐ POTTY
- ☐ CRAPPER
- ☐ WC

_____

RATINGS: 1 2 3 4 5
CLEANLINESS	☆ ☆ ☆ ☆ ☆
AMBIENCE	☆ ☆ ☆ ☆ ☆
AMENITIES	☆ ☆ ☆ ☆ ☆
SOUND PROOFING	☆ ☆ ☆ ☆ ☆
QUALITY OF THE FLUSH	☆ ☆ ☆ ☆ ☆
TOILET PAPER	☆ ☆ ☆ ☆ ☆

OVERALL EXPERIENCE:
- ☐ BEST SEAT IN THE HOUSE ★ ★ ★ ★ ★
- ☐ WOULD POOP HERE AGAIN ★ ★ ★ ★
- ☐ SHIT GOT REAL ★ ★ ★
- ☐ SAME SHIT DIFFERENT HOUSE ★ ★
- ☐ THINGS JUST DIDN'T COME OUT RIGHT ★

THOUGHTS/MESSAGES: _____
_____
_____

Welcome! PLEASE SEAT YOURSELF AND ENJOY YOUR VISIT!

NAME: _____ DATE: _____ TIME: _____ DURATION OF VISIT: _____
HRS   MIN   SEC

PURPOSE FOR VISIT: 🧻 #1 🧻 #2 🧻 OTHER: _____   SUCCESS? 🧻 YES 🧻 NO

FAVORITE EUPHEMISM FOR PERFORMING #1:

FAVORITE EUPHEMISM FOR PERFORMING #2:

FAVORITE RESTROOM GRAFFITI OR YOUR ORIGNAL DOODLE:

WHILE YOU WERE HERE, DID YOU:
☐ TEXT SOMEONE
☐ MAKE A PHONE CALL
☐ EMAIL
☐ CHECK SOCIAL MEDIA
☐ TAKE A SELFIE
☐ LOOK IN THE MEDICINE CABINET
☐ CHECK YOUR TEETH
☐ CHECK OUT YOUR BUTT
☐ CHECK YOUR FLY
☐ READ
☐ FIX YOUR HAIR
☐ TAKE SOME EXTRA "ME TIME"
☐ TALK TO YOURSELF
☐ CONDUCT BUSINESS OTHER THAN YOUR "BUSINESS." CARE TO SHARE?

FAVORITE NAME FOR THIS ROOM:
☐ BATHROOM   ☐ JOHN
☐ TOILET   ☐ CAN
☐ POWDER ROOM   ☐ HEAD
☐ LAVATORY   ☐ POTTY
☐ SHITTER   ☐ CRAPPER
☐ LOO   ☐ WC
☐ LITTLE GIRLS ROOM
☐ LITTLE BOYS ROOM
☐ COMFORT STATION
☐ OTHER: _____
_____

THOUGHTS/MESSAGES: _____
_____
_____

RATINGS:
	1	2	3	4	5
CLEANLINESS	☆	☆	☆	☆	☆
AMBIENCE	☆	☆	☆	☆	☆
AMENITIES	☆	☆	☆	☆	☆
SOUND PROOFING	☆	☆	☆	☆	☆
QUALITY OF THE FLUSH	☆	☆	☆	☆	☆
TOILET PAPER	☆	☆	☆	☆	☆

OVERALL EXPERIENCE:
☐ BEST SEAT IN THE HOUSE ★ ★ ★ ★ ★
☐ WOULD POOP HERE AGAIN ★ ★ ★ ★
☐ SHIT GOT REAL ★ ★ ★
☐ SAME SHIT DIFFERENT HOUSE ★ ★
☐ THINGS JUST DIDN'T COME OUT RIGHT ★

Welcome! PLEASE SEAT YOURSELF AND ENJOY YOUR VISIT!

NAME: _____ DATE: _____ TIME: _____ DURATION OF VISIT: _____
HRS   MIN   SEC

PURPOSE FOR VISIT: 🧻 #1 🧻 #2 🧻 OTHER: _____ SUCCESS? 🧻 YES 🧻 NO

FAVORITE EUPHEMISM FOR PERFORMING #1:

FAVORITE RESTROOM GRAFFITI OR YOUR ORIGNAL DOODLE:

FAVORITE EUPHEMISM FOR PERFORMING #2:

WHILE YOU WERE HERE, DID YOU:
- ☐ TEXT SOMEONE
- ☐ MAKE A PHONE CALL
- ☐ EMAIL
- ☐ CHECK SOCIAL MEDIA
- ☐ TAKE A SELFIE
- ☐ LOOK IN THE MEDICINE CABINET
- ☐ CHECK YOUR TEETH
- ☐ CHECK OUT YOUR BUTT
- ☐ CHECK YOUR FLY
- ☐ READ
- ☐ FIX YOUR HAIR
- ☐ TAKE SOME EXTRA "ME TIME"
- ☐ TALK TO YOURSELF
- ☐ CONDUCT BUSINESS OTHER THAN YOUR "BUSINESS." CARE TO SHARE?
  _____

FAVORITE NAME FOR THIS ROOM:
- ☐ BATHROOM
- ☐ TOILET
- ☐ POWDER ROOM
- ☐ LAVATORY
- ☐ SHITTER
- ☐ LOO
- ☐ LITTLE GIRLS ROOM
- ☐ LITTLE BOYS ROOM
- ☐ COMFORT STATION
- ☐ OTHER: _____

- ☐ JOHN
- ☐ CAN
- ☐ HEAD
- ☐ POTTY
- ☐ CRAPPER
- ☐ WC

_____

RATINGS:
	1	2	3	4	5
CLEANLINESS	☆	☆	☆	☆	☆
AMBIENCE	☆	☆	☆	☆	☆
AMENITIES	☆	☆	☆	☆	☆
SOUND PROOFING	☆	☆	☆	☆	☆
QUALITY OF THE FLUSH	☆	☆	☆	☆	☆
TOILET PAPER	☆	☆	☆	☆	☆

OVERALL EXPERIENCE:
- ☐ BEST SEAT IN THE HOUSE ★ ★ ★ ★ ★
- ☐ WOULD POOP HERE AGAIN ★ ★ ★ ★
- ☐ SHIT GOT REAL ★ ★ ★
- ☐ SAME SHIT DIFFERENT HOUSE ★ ★
- ☐ THINGS JUST DIDN'T COME OUT RIGHT ★

THOUGHTS/MESSAGES: _____
_____
_____

Welcome! PLEASE SEAT YOURSELF AND ENJOY YOUR VISIT!

NAME: _____ DATE: _____ TIME: _____ DURATION OF VISIT: _____
HRS   MIN   SEC

PURPOSE FOR VISIT: ☐ #1   ☐ #2   ☐ OTHER: _____   SUCCESS? ☐ YES ☐ NO

FAVORITE EUPHEMISM FOR PERFORMING #1:

FAVORITE RESTROOM GRAFFITI OR YOUR ORIGNAL DOODLE:

FAVORITE EUPHEMISM FOR PERFORMING #2:

WHILE YOU WERE HERE, DID YOU:

☐ TEXT SOMEONE
☐ MAKE A PHONE CALL
☐ EMAIL
☐ CHECK SOCIAL MEDIA
☐ TAKE A SELFIE
☐ LOOK IN THE MEDICINE CABINET
☐ CHECK YOUR TEETH
☐ CHECK OUT YOUR BUTT
☐ CHECK YOUR FLY
☐ READ
☐ FIX YOUR HAIR
☐ TAKE SOME EXTRA "ME TIME"
☐ TALK TO YOURSELF
☐ CONDUCT BUSINESS OTHER THAN YOUR "BUSINESS." CARE TO SHARE?

FAVORITE NAME FOR THIS ROOM:

☐ BATHROOM   ☐ JOHN
☐ TOILET   ☐ CAN
☐ POWDER ROOM   ☐ HEAD
☐ LAVATORY   ☐ POTTY
☐ SHITTER   ☐ CRAPPER
☐ LOO   ☐ WC
☐ LITTLE GIRLS ROOM
☐ LITTLE BOYS ROOM
☐ COMFORT STATION
☐ OTHER: _____
_____

THOUGHTS/MESSAGES: _____
_____
_____

RATINGS:

	1	2	3	4	5
CLEANLINESS	☆	☆	☆	☆	☆
AMBIENCE	☆	☆	☆	☆	☆
AMENITIES	☆	☆	☆	☆	☆
SOUND PROOFING	☆	☆	☆	☆	☆
QUALITY OF THE FLUSH	☆	☆	☆	☆	☆
TOILET PAPER	☆	☆	☆	☆	☆

OVERALL EXPERIENCE:

☐ BEST SEAT IN THE HOUSE ★ ★ ★ ★ ★
☐ WOULD POOP HERE AGAIN ★ ★ ★ ★
☐ SHIT GOT REAL ★ ★ ★
☐ SAME SHIT DIFFERENT HOUSE ★ ★
☐ THINGS JUST DIDN'T COME OUT RIGHT ★

Welcome! PLEASE SEAT YOURSELF AND ENJOY YOUR VISIT!

NAME: _____ DATE: _____ TIME: _____ DURATION OF VISIT: _____
HRS   MIN   SEC

PURPOSE FOR VISIT: [ ] #1   [ ] #2   [ ] OTHER: _____   SUCCESS? [ ] YES [ ] NO

FAVORITE EUPHEMISM FOR PERFORMING #1:

FAVORITE RESTROOM GRAFFITI OR YOUR ORIGNAL DOODLE:

FAVORITE EUPHEMISM FOR PERFORMING #2:

WHILE YOU WERE HERE, DID YOU:
- ☐ TEXT SOMEONE
- ☐ MAKE A PHONE CALL
- ☐ EMAIL
- ☐ CHECK SOCIAL MEDIA
- ☐ TAKE A SELFIE
- ☐ LOOK IN THE MEDICINE CABINET
- ☐ CHECK YOUR TEETH
- ☐ CHECK OUT YOUR BUTT
- ☐ CHECK YOUR FLY
- ☐ READ
- ☐ FIX YOUR HAIR
- ☐ TAKE SOME EXTRA "ME TIME"
- ☐ TALK TO YOURSELF
- ☐ CONDUCT BUSINESS OTHER THAN YOUR "BUSINESS." CARE TO SHARE?
  _____

FAVORITE NAME FOR THIS ROOM:
- ☐ BATHROOM
- ☐ TOILET
- ☐ POWDER ROOM
- ☐ LAVATORY
- ☐ SHITTER
- ☐ LOO
- ☐ LITTLE GIRLS ROOM
- ☐ LITTLE BOYS ROOM
- ☐ COMFORT STATION
- ☐ OTHER: _____
- ☐ JOHN
- ☐ CAN
- ☐ HEAD
- ☐ POTTY
- ☐ CRAPPER
- ☐ WC

_____

RATINGS: 1 2 3 4 5
CLEANLINESS   ☆ ☆ ☆ ☆ ☆
AMBIENCE   ☆ ☆ ☆ ☆ ☆
AMENITIES   ☆ ☆ ☆ ☆ ☆
SOUND PROOFING   ☆ ☆ ☆ ☆ ☆
QUALITY OF THE FLUSH   ☆ ☆ ☆ ☆ ☆
TOILET PAPER   ☆ ☆ ☆ ☆ ☆

OVERALL EXPERIENCE:
- ☐ BEST SEAT IN THE HOUSE   ★ ★ ★ ★ ★
- ☐ WOULD POOP HERE AGAIN   ★ ★ ★ ★
- ☐ SHIT GOT REAL   ★ ★ ★
- ☐ SAME SHIT DIFFERENT HOUSE   ★ ★
- ☐ THINGS JUST DIDN'T COME OUT RIGHT ★

THOUGHTS/MESSAGES: _____
_____
_____

Welcome! PLEASE SEAT YOURSELF AND ENJOY YOUR VISIT!

NAME: _____ DATE: _____ TIME: _____ DURATION OF VISIT: _____

HRS   MIN   SEC

PURPOSE FOR VISIT: ☐ #1 ☐ #2 ☐ OTHER: _____ SUCCESS? ☐ YES ☐ NO

FAVORITE EUPHEMISM FOR PERFORMING #1:

FAVORITE RESTROOM GRAFFITI OR YOUR ORIGNAL DOODLE:

FAVORITE EUPHEMISM FOR PERFORMING #2:

WHILE YOU WERE HERE, DID YOU:

☐ TEXT SOMEONE
☐ MAKE A PHONE CALL
☐ EMAIL
☐ CHECK SOCIAL MEDIA
☐ TAKE A SELFIE
☐ LOOK IN THE MEDICINE CABINET
☐ CHECK YOUR TEETH
☐ CHECK OUT YOUR BUTT
☐ CHECK YOUR FLY
☐ READ
☐ FIX YOUR HAIR
☐ TAKE SOME EXTRA "ME TIME"
☐ TALK TO YOURSELF
☐ CONDUCT BUSINESS OTHER THAN YOUR "BUSINESS." CARE TO SHARE?

FAVORITE NAME FOR THIS ROOM:

☐ BATHROOM
☐ TOILET
☐ POWDER ROOM
☐ LAVATORY
☐ SHITTER
☐ LOO
☐ LITTLE GIRLS ROOM
☐ LITTLE BOYS ROOM
☐ COMFORT STATION
☐ OTHER: _____
☐ JOHN
☐ CAN
☐ HEAD
☐ POTTY
☐ CRAPPER
☐ WC

RATINGS: 1 2 3 4 5

CLEANLINESS   ☆ ☆ ☆ ☆ ☆
AMBIENCE   ☆ ☆ ☆ ☆ ☆
AMENITIES   ☆ ☆ ☆ ☆ ☆
SOUND PROOFING   ☆ ☆ ☆ ☆ ☆
QUALITY OF THE FLUSH ☆ ☆ ☆ ☆ ☆
TOILET PAPER   ☆ ☆ ☆ ☆ ☆

OVERALL EXPERIENCE:

☐ BEST SEAT IN THE HOUSE ★ ★ ★ ★ ★
☐ WOULD POOP HERE AGAIN ★ ★ ★ ★
☐ SHIT GOT REAL ★ ★ ★
☐ SAME SHIT DIFFERENT HOUSE ★ ★
☐ THINGS JUST DIDN'T COME OUT RIGHT ★

THOUGHTS/MESSAGES: _____

Welcome! PLEASE SEAT YOURSELF AND ENJOY YOUR VISIT!

NAME: _____ DATE: _____ TIME: _____ DURATION OF VISIT: _____

HRS   MIN   SEC

PURPOSE FOR VISIT: 🧻 #1 🧻 #2 🧻 OTHER: _____   SUCCESS? 🧻 YES 🧻 NO

FAVORITE EUPHEMISM FOR PERFORMING #1:

FAVORITE EUPHEMISM FOR PERFORMING #2:

FAVORITE RESTROOM GRAFFITI OR YOUR ORIGNAL DOODLE:

WHILE YOU WERE HERE, DID YOU:

☐ TEXT SOMEONE
☐ MAKE A PHONE CALL
☐ EMAIL
☐ CHECK SOCIAL MEDIA
☐ TAKE A SELFIE
☐ LOOK IN THE MEDICINE CABINET
☐ CHECK YOUR TEETH
☐ CHECK OUT YOUR BUTT
☐ CHECK YOUR FLY
☐ READ
☐ FIX YOUR HAIR
☐ TAKE SOME EXTRA "ME TIME"
☐ TALK TO YOURSELF
☐ CONDUCT BUSINESS OTHER THAN YOUR "BUSINESS." CARE TO SHARE?

_____

FAVORITE NAME FOR THIS ROOM:

☐ BATHROOM   ☐ JOHN
☐ TOILET   ☐ CAN
☐ POWDER ROOM   ☐ HEAD
☐ LAVATORY   ☐ POTTY
☐ SHITTER   ☐ CRAPPER
☐ LOO   ☐ WC
☐ LITTLE GIRLS ROOM
☐ LITTLE BOYS ROOM
☐ COMFORT STATION
☐ OTHER: _____

_____

THOUGHTS/MESSAGES: _____

_____

_____

RATINGS: 1 2 3 4 5

CLEANLINESS   ☆ ☆ ☆ ☆ ☆
AMBIENCE   ☆ ☆ ☆ ☆ ☆
AMENITIES   ☆ ☆ ☆ ☆ ☆
SOUND PROOFING   ☆ ☆ ☆ ☆ ☆
QUALITY OF THE FLUSH ☆ ☆ ☆ ☆ ☆
TOILET PAPER   ☆ ☆ ☆ ☆ ☆

OVERALL EXPERIENCE:

☐ BEST SEAT IN THE HOUSE   ★ ★ ★ ★ ★
☐ WOULD POOP HERE AGAIN   ★ ★ ★ ★
☐ SHIT GOT REAL   ★ ★ ★
☐ SAME SHIT DIFFERENT HOUSE   ★ ★
☐ THINGS JUST DIDN'T COME OUT RIGHT ★

Welcome! PLEASE SEAT YOURSELF AND ENJOY YOUR VISIT!

NAME: _____ DATE: _____ TIME: _____ DURATION OF VISIT: _____
HRS   MIN   SEC

PURPOSE FOR VISIT: 🧻 #1 🧻 #2 🧻 OTHER: _____ SUCCESS? 🧻 YES 🧻 NO

FAVORITE EUPHEMISM FOR PERFORMING #1:

FAVORITE EUPHEMISM FOR PERFORMING #2:

FAVORITE RESTROOM GRAFFITI OR YOUR ORIGNAL DOODLE:

WHILE YOU WERE HERE, DID YOU:
- ☐ TEXT SOMEONE
- ☐ MAKE A PHONE CALL
- ☐ EMAIL
- ☐ CHECK SOCIAL MEDIA
- ☐ TAKE A SELFIE
- ☐ LOOK IN THE MEDICINE CABINET
- ☐ CHECK YOUR TEETH
- ☐ CHECK OUT YOUR BUTT
- ☐ CHECK YOUR FLY
- ☐ READ
- ☐ FIX YOUR HAIR
- ☐ TAKE SOME EXTRA "ME TIME"
- ☐ TALK TO YOURSELF
- ☐ CONDUCT BUSINESS OTHER THAN YOUR "BUSINESS." CARE TO SHARE?

FAVORITE NAME FOR THIS ROOM:
- ☐ BATHROOM
- ☐ TOILET
- ☐ POWDER ROOM
- ☐ LAVATORY
- ☐ SHITTER
- ☐ LOO
- ☐ LITTLE GIRLS ROOM
- ☐ LITTLE BOYS ROOM
- ☐ COMFORT STATION
- ☐ OTHER: _____
- ☐ JOHN
- ☐ CAN
- ☐ HEAD
- ☐ POTTY
- ☐ CRAPPER
- ☐ WC

RATINGS:

	1	2	3	4	5
CLEANLINESS	☆	☆	☆	☆	☆
AMBIENCE	☆	☆	☆	☆	☆
AMENITIES	☆	☆	☆	☆	☆
SOUND PROOFING	☆	☆	☆	☆	☆
QUALITY OF THE FLUSH	☆	☆	☆	☆	☆
TOILET PAPER	☆	☆	☆	☆	☆

OVERALL EXPERIENCE:
- ☐ BEST SEAT IN THE HOUSE   ★ ★ ★ ★ ★
- ☐ WOULD POOP HERE AGAIN   ★ ★ ★ ★
- ☐ SHIT GOT REAL   ★ ★ ★
- ☐ SAME SHIT DIFFERENT HOUSE   ★ ★
- ☐ THINGS JUST DIDN'T COME OUT RIGHT   ★

THOUGHTS/MESSAGES: _____

Welcome! PLEASE SEAT YOURSELF AND ENJOY YOUR VISIT!

NAME: _____ DATE: _____ TIME: _____ DURATION OF VISIT: _____
HRS   MIN   SEC

PURPOSE FOR VISIT: 🧻 #1   🧻 #2   🧻 OTHER: _____   SUCCESS? 🧻 YES 🧻 NO

FAVORITE EUPHEMISM FOR PERFORMING #1:

FAVORITE EUPHEMISM FOR PERFORMING #2:

FAVORITE RESTROOM GRAFFITI OR YOUR ORIGNAL DOODLE:

WHILE YOU WERE HERE, DID YOU:
☐ TEXT SOMEONE
☐ MAKE A PHONE CALL
☐ EMAIL
☐ CHECK SOCIAL MEDIA
☐ TAKE A SELFIE
☐ LOOK IN THE MEDICINE CABINET
☐ CHECK YOUR TEETH
☐ CHECK OUT YOUR BUTT
☐ CHECK YOUR FLY
☐ READ
☐ FIX YOUR HAIR
☐ TAKE SOME EXTRA "ME TIME"
☐ TALK TO YOURSELF
☐ CONDUCT BUSINESS OTHER THAN YOUR "BUSINESS." CARE TO SHARE?

FAVORITE NAME FOR THIS ROOM:
☐ BATHROOM   ☐ JOHN
☐ TOILET   ☐ CAN
☐ POWDER ROOM   ☐ HEAD
☐ LAVATORY   ☐ POTTY
☐ SHITTER   ☐ CRAPPER
☐ LOO   ☐ WC
☐ LITTLE GIRLS ROOM
☐ LITTLE BOYS ROOM
☐ COMFORT STATION
☐ OTHER: _____

_____

RATINGS: 1 2 3 4 5
CLEANLINESS   ☆ ☆ ☆ ☆ ☆
AMBIENCE   ☆ ☆ ☆ ☆ ☆
AMENITIES   ☆ ☆ ☆ ☆ ☆
SOUND PROOFING   ☆ ☆ ☆ ☆ ☆
QUALITY OF THE FLUSH ☆ ☆ ☆ ☆ ☆
TOILET PAPER   ☆ ☆ ☆ ☆ ☆

OVERALL EXPERIENCE:
☐ BEST SEAT IN THE HOUSE   ★ ★ ★ ★ ★
☐ WOULD POOP HERE AGAIN   ★ ★ ★ ★
☐ SHIT GOT REAL   ★ ★ ★
☐ SAME SHIT DIFFERENT HOUSE   ★ ★
☐ THINGS JUST DIDN'T COME OUT RIGHT ★

THOUGHTS/MESSAGES: _____

_____

Welcome! PLEASE SEAT YOURSELF AND ENJOY YOUR VISIT!

NAME: _____ DATE: _____ TIME: _____ DURATION OF VISIT: _____
HRS   MIN   SEC

PURPOSE FOR VISIT: ☐ #1 ☐ #2 ☐ OTHER: _____ SUCCESS? ☐ YES ☐ NO

FAVORITE EUPHEMISM FOR PERFORMING #1: | FAVORITE RESTROOM GRAFFITI OR YOUR ORIGNAL DOODLE:

FAVORITE EUPHEMISM FOR PERFORMING #2:

WHILE YOU WERE HERE, DID YOU:
☐ TEXT SOMEONE
☐ MAKE A PHONE CALL
☐ EMAIL
☐ CHECK SOCIAL MEDIA
☐ TAKE A SELFIE
☐ LOOK IN THE MEDICINE CABINET
☐ CHECK YOUR TEETH
☐ CHECK OUT YOUR BUTT
☐ CHECK YOUR FLY
☐ READ
☐ FIX YOUR HAIR
☐ TAKE SOME EXTRA "ME TIME"
☐ TALK TO YOURSELF
☐ CONDUCT BUSINESS OTHER THAN YOUR "BUSINESS." CARE TO SHARE?

FAVORITE NAME FOR THIS ROOM:
☐ BATHROOM   ☐ JOHN
☐ TOILET   ☐ CAN
☐ POWDER ROOM   ☐ HEAD
☐ LAVATORY   ☐ POTTY
☐ SHITTER   ☐ CRAPPER
☐ LOO   ☐ WC
☐ LITTLE GIRLS ROOM
☐ LITTLE BOYS ROOM
☐ COMFORT STATION
☐ OTHER: _____
_____

RATINGS:
	1	2	3	4	5
CLEANLINESS	☆	☆	☆	☆	☆
AMBIENCE	☆	☆	☆	☆	☆
AMENITIES	☆	☆	☆	☆	☆
SOUND PROOFING	☆	☆	☆	☆	☆
QUALITY OF THE FLUSH	☆	☆	☆	☆	☆
TOILET PAPER	☆	☆	☆	☆	☆

OVERALL EXPERIENCE:
☐ BEST SEAT IN THE HOUSE ★ ★ ★ ★ ★
☐ WOULD POOP HERE AGAIN ★ ★ ★ ★
☐ SHIT GOT REAL ★ ★ ★
☐ SAME SHIT DIFFERENT HOUSE ★ ★
☐ THINGS JUST DIDN'T COME OUT RIGHT ★

THOUGHTS/MESSAGES: _____
_____
_____

Welcome! PLEASE SEAT YOURSELF AND ENJOY YOUR VISIT!

NAME: _____ DATE: _____ TIME: _____ DURATION OF VISIT: _____
HRS   MIN   SEC

PURPOSE FOR VISIT: 🧻 #1   🧻 #2   🧻 OTHER: _____   SUCCESS? 🧻 YES 🧻 NO

FAVORITE EUPHEMISM FOR PERFORMING #1:

FAVORITE RESTROOM GRAFFITI OR YOUR ORIGNAL DOODLE:

FAVORITE EUPHEMISM FOR PERFORMING #2:

WHILE YOU WERE HERE, DID YOU:
☐ TEXT SOMEONE
☐ MAKE A PHONE CALL
☐ EMAIL
☐ CHECK SOCIAL MEDIA
☐ TAKE A SELFIE
☐ LOOK IN THE MEDICINE CABINET
☐ CHECK YOUR TEETH
☐ CHECK OUT YOUR BUTT
☐ CHECK YOUR FLY
☐ READ
☐ FIX YOUR HAIR
☐ TAKE SOME EXTRA "ME TIME"
☐ TALK TO YOURSELF
☐ CONDUCT BUSINESS OTHER THAN YOUR "BUSINESS." CARE TO SHARE?
_____

FAVORITE NAME FOR THIS ROOM:
☐ BATHROOM   ☐ JOHN
☐ TOILET   ☐ CAN
☐ POWDER ROOM   ☐ HEAD
☐ LAVATORY   ☐ POTTY
☐ SHITTER   ☐ CRAPPER
☐ LOO   ☐ WC
☐ LITTLE GIRLS ROOM
☐ LITTLE BOYS ROOM
☐ COMFORT STATION
☐ OTHER: _____
_____
_____

THOUGHTS/MESSAGES: _____
_____
_____

RATINGS:
	1	2	3	4	5
CLEANLINESS	☆	☆	☆	☆	☆
AMBIENCE	☆	☆	☆	☆	☆
AMENITIES	☆	☆	☆	☆	☆
SOUND PROOFING	☆	☆	☆	☆	☆
QUALITY OF THE FLUSH	☆	☆	☆	☆	☆
TOILET PAPER	☆	☆	☆	☆	☆

OVERALL EXPERIENCE:
☐ BEST SEAT IN THE HOUSE   ★ ★ ★ ★ ★
☐ WOULD POOP HERE AGAIN   ★ ★ ★ ★
☐ SHIT GOT REAL   ★ ★ ★
☐ SAME SHIT DIFFERENT HOUSE   ★ ★
☐ THINGS JUST DIDN'T COME OUT RIGHT ★

Welcome! PLEASE SEAT YOURSELF AND ENJOY YOUR VISIT!

NAME: _____ DATE: _____ TIME: _____ DURATION OF VISIT: _____
HRS   MIN   SEC

PURPOSE FOR VISIT: 🧻 #1 🧻 #2 🧻 OTHER: _____   SUCCESS? 🧻 YES 🧻 NO

FAVORITE EUPHEMISM FOR PERFORMING #1:

FAVORITE EUPHEMISM FOR PERFORMING #2:

FAVORITE RESTROOM GRAFFITI OR YOUR ORIGNAL DOODLE:

WHILE YOU WERE HERE, DID YOU:
- ☐ TEXT SOMEONE
- ☐ MAKE A PHONE CALL
- ☐ EMAIL
- ☐ CHECK SOCIAL MEDIA
- ☐ TAKE A SELFIE
- ☐ LOOK IN THE MEDICINE CABINET
- ☐ CHECK YOUR TEETH
- ☐ CHECK OUT YOUR BUTT
- ☐ CHECK YOUR FLY
- ☐ READ
- ☐ FIX YOUR HAIR
- ☐ TAKE SOME EXTRA "ME TIME"
- ☐ TALK TO YOURSELF
- ☐ CONDUCT BUSINESS OTHER THAN YOUR "BUSINESS." CARE TO SHARE?

FAVORITE NAME FOR THIS ROOM:
- ☐ BATHROOM
- ☐ TOILET
- ☐ POWDER ROOM
- ☐ LAVATORY
- ☐ SHITTER
- ☐ LOO
- ☐ LITTLE GIRLS ROOM
- ☐ LITTLE BOYS ROOM
- ☐ COMFORT STATION
- ☐ OTHER: _____
- ☐ JOHN
- ☐ CAN
- ☐ HEAD
- ☐ POTTY
- ☐ CRAPPER
- ☐ WC

RATINGS:
	1 2 3 4 5
CLEANLINESS	☆ ☆ ☆ ☆ ☆
AMBIENCE	☆ ☆ ☆ ☆ ☆
AMENITIES	☆ ☆ ☆ ☆ ☆
SOUND PROOFING	☆ ☆ ☆ ☆ ☆
QUALITY OF THE FLUSH	☆ ☆ ☆ ☆ ☆
TOILET PAPER	☆ ☆ ☆ ☆ ☆

OVERALL EXPERIENCE:
- ☐ BEST SEAT IN THE HOUSE ★ ★ ★ ★ ★
- ☐ WOULD POOP HERE AGAIN ★ ★ ★ ★
- ☐ SHIT GOT REAL ★ ★ ★
- ☐ SAME SHIT DIFFERENT HOUSE ★ ★
- ☐ THINGS JUST DIDN'T COME OUT RIGHT ★

THOUGHTS/MESSAGES: _____

Welcome! PLEASE SEAT YOURSELF AND ENJOY YOUR VISIT!

NAME: _____ DATE: _____ TIME: _____ DURATION OF VISIT: _____

HRS   MIN   SEC

PURPOSE FOR VISIT: ☐ #1 ☐ #2 ☐ OTHER: _____ SUCCESS? ☐ YES ☐ NO

FAVORITE EUPHEMISM FOR PERFORMING #1:

FAVORITE RESTROOM GRAFFITI OR YOUR ORIGNAL DOODLE:

FAVORITE EUPHEMISM FOR PERFORMING #2:

WHILE YOU WERE HERE, DID YOU:

☐ TEXT SOMEONE
☐ MAKE A PHONE CALL
☐ EMAIL
☐ CHECK SOCIAL MEDIA
☐ TAKE A SELFIE
☐ LOOK IN THE MEDICINE CABINET
☐ CHECK YOUR TEETH
☐ CHECK OUT YOUR BUTT
☐ CHECK YOUR FLY
☐ READ
☐ FIX YOUR HAIR
☐ TAKE SOME EXTRA "ME TIME"
☐ TALK TO YOURSELF
☐ CONDUCT BUSINESS OTHER THAN YOUR "BUSINESS." CARE TO SHARE?
_____

FAVORITE NAME FOR THIS ROOM:

☐ BATHROOM   ☐ JOHN
☐ TOILET   ☐ CAN
☐ POWDER ROOM   ☐ HEAD
☐ LAVATORY   ☐ POTTY
☐ SHITTER   ☐ CRAPPER
☐ LOO   ☐ WC
☐ LITTLE GIRLS ROOM
☐ LITTLE BOYS ROOM
☐ COMFORT STATION
☐ OTHER: _____

_____

RATINGS:

	1	2	3	4	5
CLEANLINESS	☆	☆	☆	☆	☆
AMBIENCE	☆	☆	☆	☆	☆
AMENITIES	☆	☆	☆	☆	☆
SOUND PROOFING	☆	☆	☆	☆	☆
QUALITY OF THE FLUSH	☆	☆	☆	☆	☆
TOILET PAPER	☆	☆	☆	☆	☆

OVERALL EXPERIENCE:

☐ BEST SEAT IN THE HOUSE   ★ ★ ★ ★ ★
☐ WOULD POOP HERE AGAIN   ★ ★ ★ ★
☐ SHIT GOT REAL   ★ ★ ★
☐ SAME SHIT DIFFERENT HOUSE   ★ ★
☐ THINGS JUST DIDN'T COME OUT RIGHT   ★

THOUGHTS/MESSAGES: _____
_____
_____

Welcome! PLEASE SEAT YOURSELF AND ENJOY YOUR VISIT!

NAME: _____ DATE: _____ TIME: _____ DURATION OF VISIT: _____
HRS   MIN   SEC

PURPOSE FOR VISIT: ☐ #1 ☐ #2 ☐ OTHER: _____ SUCCESS? ☐ YES ☐ NO

FAVORITE EUPHEMISM FOR PERFORMING #1:

FAVORITE RESTROOM GRAFFITI OR YOUR ORIGNAL DOODLE:

FAVORITE EUPHEMISM FOR PERFORMING #2:

WHILE YOU WERE HERE, DID YOU:
- ☐ TEXT SOMEONE
- ☐ MAKE A PHONE CALL
- ☐ EMAIL
- ☐ CHECK SOCIAL MEDIA
- ☐ TAKE A SELFIE
- ☐ LOOK IN THE MEDICINE CABINET
- ☐ CHECK YOUR TEETH
- ☐ CHECK OUT YOUR BUTT
- ☐ CHECK YOUR FLY
- ☐ READ
- ☐ FIX YOUR HAIR
- ☐ TAKE SOME EXTRA "ME TIME"
- ☐ TALK TO YOURSELF
- ☐ CONDUCT BUSINESS OTHER THAN YOUR "BUSINESS." CARE TO SHARE?
  _____

FAVORITE NAME FOR THIS ROOM:
- ☐ BATHROOM
- ☐ TOILET
- ☐ POWDER ROOM
- ☐ LAVATORY
- ☐ SHITTER
- ☐ LOO
- ☐ LITTLE GIRLS ROOM
- ☐ LITTLE BOYS ROOM
- ☐ COMFORT STATION
- ☐ OTHER: _____
- ☐ JOHN
- ☐ CAN
- ☐ HEAD
- ☐ POTTY
- ☐ CRAPPER
- ☐ WC

_____

THOUGHTS/MESSAGES: _____
_____
_____

RATINGS:

	1	2	3	4	5
CLEANLINESS	☆	☆	☆	☆	☆
AMBIENCE	☆	☆	☆	☆	☆
AMENITIES	☆	☆	☆	☆	☆
SOUND PROOFING	☆	☆	☆	☆	☆
QUALITY OF THE FLUSH	☆	☆	☆	☆	☆
TOILET PAPER	☆	☆	☆	☆	☆

OVERALL EXPERIENCE:
- ☐ BEST SEAT IN THE HOUSE ★ ★ ★ ★ ★
- ☐ WOULD POOP HERE AGAIN ★ ★ ★ ★
- ☐ SHIT GOT REAL ★ ★ ★
- ☐ SAME SHIT DIFFERENT HOUSE ★ ★
- ☐ THINGS JUST DIDN'T COME OUT RIGHT ★

Welcome! PLEASE SEAT YOURSELF AND ENJOY YOUR VISIT!

NAME: _____ DATE: _____ TIME: _____ DURATION OF VISIT: _____
                                                                        HRS MIN SEC

PURPOSE FOR VISIT: 🧻 #1 🧻 #2 🧻 OTHER: _____ SUCCESS? 🧻 YES 🧻 NO

FAVORITE EUPHEMISM FOR PERFORMING #1: | FAVORITE RESTROOM GRAFFITI OR YOUR ORIGNAL DOODLE:

FAVORITE EUPHEMISM FOR PERFORMING #2:

WHILE YOU WERE HERE, DID YOU:
- ☐ TEXT SOMEONE
- ☐ MAKE A PHONE CALL
- ☐ EMAIL
- ☐ CHECK SOCIAL MEDIA
- ☐ TAKE A SELFIE
- ☐ LOOK IN THE MEDICINE CABINET
- ☐ CHECK YOUR TEETH
- ☐ CHECK OUT YOUR BUTT
- ☐ CHECK YOUR FLY
- ☐ READ
- ☐ FIX YOUR HAIR
- ☐ TAKE SOME EXTRA "ME TIME"
- ☐ TALK TO YOURSELF
- ☐ CONDUCT BUSINESS OTHER THAN YOUR "BUSINESS." CARE TO SHARE?
_____

FAVORITE NAME FOR THIS ROOM:
- ☐ BATHROOM
- ☐ TOILET
- ☐ POWDER ROOM
- ☐ LAVATORY
- ☐ SHITTER
- ☐ LOO
- ☐ LITTLE GIRLS ROOM
- ☐ LITTLE BOYS ROOM
- ☐ COMFORT STATION
- ☐ OTHER: _____
- ☐ JOHN
- ☐ CAN
- ☐ HEAD
- ☐ POTTY
- ☐ CRAPPER
- ☐ WC

_____

RATINGS:	1	2	3	4	5
CLEANLINESS	☆	☆	☆	☆	☆
AMBIENCE	☆	☆	☆	☆	☆
AMENITIES	☆	☆	☆	☆	☆
SOUND PROOFING	☆	☆	☆	☆	☆
QUALITY OF THE FLUSH	☆	☆	☆	☆	☆
TOILET PAPER	☆	☆	☆	☆	☆

OVERALL EXPERIENCE:
- ☐ BEST SEAT IN THE HOUSE ★★★★★
- ☐ WOULD POOP HERE AGAIN ★★★★
- ☐ SHIT GOT REAL ★★★
- ☐ SAME SHIT DIFFERENT HOUSE ★★
- ☐ THINGS JUST DIDN'T COME OUT RIGHT ★

THOUGHTS/MESSAGES: _____
_____
_____

Welcome! PLEASE SEAT YOURSELF AND ENJOY YOUR VISIT!

NAME: _____ DATE: _____ TIME: _____ DURATION OF VISIT: _____
HRS   MIN   SEC

PURPOSE FOR VISIT: 🧻 #1 🧻 #2 🧻 OTHER: _____ SUCCESS? 🧻 YES 🧻 NO

FAVORITE EUPHEMISM FOR PERFORMING #1:

FAVORITE EUPHEMISM FOR PERFORMING #2:

FAVORITE RESTROOM GRAFFITI OR YOUR ORIGNAL DOODLE:

WHILE YOU WERE HERE, DID YOU:
☐ TEXT SOMEONE
☐ MAKE A PHONE CALL
☐ EMAIL
☐ CHECK SOCIAL MEDIA
☐ TAKE A SELFIE
☐ LOOK IN THE MEDICINE CABINET
☐ CHECK YOUR TEETH
☐ CHECK OUT YOUR BUTT
☐ CHECK YOUR FLY
☐ READ
☐ FIX YOUR HAIR
☐ TAKE SOME EXTRA "ME TIME"
☐ TALK TO YOURSELF
☐ CONDUCT BUSINESS OTHER THAN YOUR "BUSINESS." CARE TO SHARE?

FAVORITE NAME FOR THIS ROOM:
☐ BATHROOM   ☐ JOHN
☐ TOILET   ☐ CAN
☐ POWDER ROOM   ☐ HEAD
☐ LAVATORY   ☐ POTTY
☐ SHITTER   ☐ CRAPPER
☐ LOO   ☐ WC
☐ LITTLE GIRLS ROOM
☐ LITTLE BOYS ROOM
☐ COMFORT STATION
☐ OTHER: _____

RATINGS: 1 2 3 4 5
CLEANLINESS   ☆ ☆ ☆ ☆ ☆
AMBIENCE   ☆ ☆ ☆ ☆ ☆
AMENITIES   ☆ ☆ ☆ ☆ ☆
SOUND PROOFING   ☆ ☆ ☆ ☆ ☆
QUALITY OF THE FLUSH   ☆ ☆ ☆ ☆ ☆
TOILET PAPER   ☆ ☆ ☆ ☆ ☆

OVERALL EXPERIENCE:
☐ BEST SEAT IN THE HOUSE   ★ ★ ★ ★ ★
☐ WOULD POOP HERE AGAIN   ★ ★ ★ ★
☐ SHIT GOT REAL   ★ ★ ★
☐ SAME SHIT DIFFERENT HOUSE   ★ ★
☐ THINGS JUST DIDN'T COME OUT RIGHT ★

THOUGHTS/MESSAGES: _____
_____
_____

Welcome! PLEASE SEAT YOURSELF AND ENJOY YOUR VISIT!

NAME: _____ DATE: _____ TIME: _____ DURATION OF VISIT: _____
HRS   MIN   SEC

PURPOSE FOR VISIT: 🧻 #1 🧻 #2 🧻 OTHER: _____ SUCCESS? 🧻 YES 🧻 NO

FAVORITE EUPHEMISM FOR PERFORMING #1:

FAVORITE RESTROOM GRAFFITI OR YOUR ORIGNAL DOODLE:

FAVORITE EUPHEMISM FOR PERFORMING #2:

WHILE YOU WERE HERE, DID YOU:
- ☐ TEXT SOMEONE
- ☐ MAKE A PHONE CALL
- ☐ EMAIL
- ☐ CHECK SOCIAL MEDIA
- ☐ TAKE A SELFIE
- ☐ LOOK IN THE MEDICINE CABINET
- ☐ CHECK YOUR TEETH
- ☐ CHECK OUT YOUR BUTT
- ☐ CHECK YOUR FLY
- ☐ READ
- ☐ FIX YOUR HAIR
- ☐ TAKE SOME EXTRA "ME TIME"
- ☐ TALK TO YOURSELF
- ☐ CONDUCT BUSINESS OTHER THAN YOUR "BUSINESS." CARE TO SHARE?
  _____

FAVORITE NAME FOR THIS ROOM:
- ☐ BATHROOM
- ☐ TOILET
- ☐ POWDER ROOM
- ☐ LAVATORY
- ☐ SHITTER
- ☐ LOO
- ☐ LITTLE GIRLS ROOM
- ☐ LITTLE BOYS ROOM
- ☐ COMFORT STATION
- ☐ OTHER: _____
- ☐ JOHN
- ☐ CAN
- ☐ HEAD
- ☐ POTTY
- ☐ CRAPPER
- ☐ WC

_____

RATINGS:
	1	2	3	4	5
CLEANLINESS	☆	☆	☆	☆	☆
AMBIENCE	☆	☆	☆	☆	☆
AMENITIES	☆	☆	☆	☆	☆
SOUND PROOFING	☆	☆	☆	☆	☆
QUALITY OF THE FLUSH	☆	☆	☆	☆	☆
TOILET PAPER	☆	☆	☆	☆	☆

OVERALL EXPERIENCE:
- ☐ BEST SEAT IN THE HOUSE ★ ★ ★ ★ ★
- ☐ WOULD POOP HERE AGAIN ★ ★ ★ ★
- ☐ SHIT GOT REAL ★ ★ ★
- ☐ SAME SHIT DIFFERENT HOUSE ★ ★
- ☐ THINGS JUST DIDN'T COME OUT RIGHT ★

THOUGHTS/MESSAGES: _____
_____
_____

Welcome! PLEASE SEAT YOURSELF AND ENJOY YOUR VISIT!

NAME: _____   DATE: _____   TIME: _____   DURATION OF VISIT: _____
                                                                                    HRS   MIN   SEC

PURPOSE FOR VISIT: 🧻 #1 🧻 #2 🧻 OTHER: _____   SUCCESS? 🧻 YES 🧻 NO

FAVORITE EUPHEMISM FOR PERFORMING #1: _____

FAVORITE RESTROOM GRAFFITI OR YOUR ORIGNAL DOODLE:

FAVORITE EUPHEMISM FOR PERFORMING #2: _____

WHILE YOU WERE HERE, DID YOU:
- ☐ TEXT SOMEONE
- ☐ MAKE A PHONE CALL
- ☐ EMAIL
- ☐ CHECK SOCIAL MEDIA
- ☐ TAKE A SELFIE
- ☐ LOOK IN THE MEDICINE CABINET
- ☐ CHECK YOUR TEETH
- ☐ CHECK OUT YOUR BUTT
- ☐ CHECK YOUR FLY
- ☐ READ
- ☐ FIX YOUR HAIR
- ☐ TAKE SOME EXTRA "ME TIME"
- ☐ TALK TO YOURSELF
- ☐ CONDUCT BUSINESS OTHER THAN YOUR "BUSINESS." CARE TO SHARE?

FAVORITE NAME FOR THIS ROOM:
- ☐ BATHROOM
- ☐ TOILET
- ☐ POWDER ROOM
- ☐ LAVATORY
- ☐ SHITTER
- ☐ LOO
- ☐ LITTLE GIRLS ROOM
- ☐ LITTLE BOYS ROOM
- ☐ COMFORT STATION
- ☐ OTHER: _____
- ☐ JOHN
- ☐ CAN
- ☐ HEAD
- ☐ POTTY
- ☐ CRAPPER
- ☐ WC

THOUGHTS/MESSAGES: _____
_____
_____

RATINGS: 1 2 3 4 5
CLEANLINESS   ☆ ☆ ☆ ☆ ☆
AMBIENCE   ☆ ☆ ☆ ☆ ☆
AMENITIES   ☆ ☆ ☆ ☆ ☆
SOUND PROOFING   ☆ ☆ ☆ ☆ ☆
QUALITY OF THE FLUSH ☆ ☆ ☆ ☆ ☆
TOILET PAPER   ☆ ☆ ☆ ☆ ☆

OVERALL EXPERIENCE:
- ☐ BEST SEAT IN THE HOUSE   ★ ★ ★ ★ ★
- ☐ WOULD POOP HERE AGAIN   ★ ★ ★ ★
- ☐ SHIT GOT REAL   ★ ★ ★
- ☐ SAME SHIT DIFFERENT HOUSE   ★ ★
- ☐ THINGS JUST DIDN'T COME OUT RIGHT ★

Welcome! PLEASE SEAT YOURSELF AND ENJOY YOUR VISIT!

NAME: _____ DATE: _____ TIME: _____ DURATION OF VISIT: _____
HRS   MIN   SEC

PURPOSE FOR VISIT: 🧻 #1 🧻 #2 🧻 OTHER: _____ SUCCESS? 🧻 YES 🧻 NO

FAVORITE EUPHEMISM FOR PERFORMING #1:

FAVORITE RESTROOM GRAFFITI OR YOUR ORIGNAL DOODLE:

FAVORITE EUPHEMISM FOR PERFORMING #2:

WHILE YOU WERE HERE, DID YOU:
- ☐ TEXT SOMEONE
- ☐ MAKE A PHONE CALL
- ☐ EMAIL
- ☐ CHECK SOCIAL MEDIA
- ☐ TAKE A SELFIE
- ☐ LOOK IN THE MEDICINE CABINET
- ☐ CHECK YOUR TEETH
- ☐ CHECK OUT YOUR BUTT
- ☐ CHECK YOUR FLY
- ☐ READ
- ☐ FIX YOUR HAIR
- ☐ TAKE SOME EXTRA "ME TIME"
- ☐ TALK TO YOURSELF
- ☐ CONDUCT BUSINESS OTHER THAN YOUR "BUSINESS." CARE TO SHARE?

_____

FAVORITE NAME FOR THIS ROOM:
- ☐ BATHROOM
- ☐ TOILET
- ☐ POWDER ROOM
- ☐ LAVATORY
- ☐ SHITTER
- ☐ LOO
- ☐ LITTLE GIRLS ROOM
- ☐ LITTLE BOYS ROOM
- ☐ COMFORT STATION
- ☐ OTHER: _____

- ☐ JOHN
- ☐ CAN
- ☐ HEAD
- ☐ POTTY
- ☐ CRAPPER
- ☐ WC

_____

RATINGS:
	1	2	3	4	5
CLEANLINESS	☆	☆	☆	☆	☆
AMBIENCE	☆	☆	☆	☆	☆
AMENITIES	☆	☆	☆	☆	☆
SOUND PROOFING	☆	☆	☆	☆	☆
QUALITY OF THE FLUSH	☆	☆	☆	☆	☆
TOILET PAPER	☆	☆	☆	☆	☆

OVERALL EXPERIENCE:
- ☐ BEST SEAT IN THE HOUSE ★ ★ ★ ★ ★
- ☐ WOULD POOP HERE AGAIN ★ ★ ★ ★
- ☐ SHIT GOT REAL ★ ★ ★
- ☐ SAME SHIT DIFFERENT HOUSE ★ ★
- ☐ THINGS JUST DIDN'T COME OUT RIGHT ★

THOUGHTS/MESSAGES: _____
_____
_____

Welcome! PLEASE SEAT YOURSELF AND ENJOY YOUR VISIT!

NAME: _____ DATE: _____ TIME: _____ DURATION OF VISIT: _____
HRS   MIN   SEC

PURPOSE FOR VISIT: 🧻 #1 🧻 #2 🧻 OTHER: _____ SUCCESS? 🧻 YES 🧻 NO

FAVORITE EUPHEMISM FOR PERFORMING #1:

FAVORITE RESTROOM GRAFFITI OR YOUR ORIGNAL DOODLE:

FAVORITE EUPHEMISM FOR PERFORMING #2:

WHILE YOU WERE HERE, DID YOU:
- ☐ TEXT SOMEONE
- ☐ MAKE A PHONE CALL
- ☐ EMAIL
- ☐ CHECK SOCIAL MEDIA
- ☐ TAKE A SELFIE
- ☐ LOOK IN THE MEDICINE CABINET
- ☐ CHECK YOUR TEETH
- ☐ CHECK OUT YOUR BUTT
- ☐ CHECK YOUR FLY
- ☐ READ
- ☐ FIX YOUR HAIR
- ☐ TAKE SOME EXTRA "ME TIME"
- ☐ TALK TO YOURSELF
- ☐ CONDUCT BUSINESS OTHER THAN YOUR "BUSINESS." CARE TO SHARE?
  _____

FAVORITE NAME FOR THIS ROOM:
- ☐ BATHROOM
- ☐ TOILET
- ☐ POWDER ROOM
- ☐ LAVATORY
- ☐ SHITTER
- ☐ LOO
- ☐ LITTLE GIRLS ROOM
- ☐ LITTLE BOYS ROOM
- ☐ COMFORT STATION
- ☐ OTHER: _____
- ☐ JOHN
- ☐ CAN
- ☐ HEAD
- ☐ POTTY
- ☐ CRAPPER
- ☐ WC

_____

RATINGS:
	1	2	3	4	5
CLEANLINESS	☆	☆	☆	☆	☆
AMBIENCE	☆	☆	☆	☆	☆
AMENITIES	☆	☆	☆	☆	☆
SOUND PROOFING	☆	☆	☆	☆	☆
QUALITY OF THE FLUSH	☆	☆	☆	☆	☆
TOILET PAPER	☆	☆	☆	☆	☆

OVERALL EXPERIENCE:
- ☐ BEST SEAT IN THE HOUSE ★ ★ ★ ★ ★
- ☐ WOULD POOP HERE AGAIN ★ ★ ★ ★
- ☐ SHIT GOT REAL ★ ★ ★
- ☐ SAME SHIT DIFFERENT HOUSE ★ ★
- ☐ THINGS JUST DIDN'T COME OUT RIGHT ★

THOUGHTS/MESSAGES: _____
_____
_____

Welcome! PLEASE SEAT YOURSELF AND ENJOY YOUR VISIT!

NAME: _____ DATE: _____ TIME: _____ DURATION OF VISIT: _____
HRS   MIN   SEC

PURPOSE FOR VISIT: ☐ #1 ☐ #2 ☐ OTHER: _____ SUCCESS? ☐ YES ☐ NO

FAVORITE EUPHEMISM FOR PERFORMING #1:

FAVORITE RESTROOM GRAFFITI OR YOUR ORIGNAL DOODLE:

FAVORITE EUPHEMISM FOR PERFORMING #2:

WHILE YOU WERE HERE, DID YOU:
- ☐ TEXT SOMEONE
- ☐ MAKE A PHONE CALL
- ☐ EMAIL
- ☐ CHECK SOCIAL MEDIA
- ☐ TAKE A SELFIE
- ☐ LOOK IN THE MEDICINE CABINET
- ☐ CHECK YOUR TEETH
- ☐ CHECK OUT YOUR BUTT
- ☐ CHECK YOUR FLY
- ☐ READ
- ☐ FIX YOUR HAIR
- ☐ TAKE SOME EXTRA "ME TIME"
- ☐ TALK TO YOURSELF
- ☐ CONDUCT BUSINESS OTHER THAN YOUR "BUSINESS." CARE TO SHARE?
  _____

FAVORITE NAME FOR THIS ROOM:
- ☐ BATHROOM
- ☐ TOILET
- ☐ POWDER ROOM
- ☐ LAVATORY
- ☐ SHITTER
- ☐ LOO
- ☐ LITTLE GIRLS ROOM
- ☐ LITTLE BOYS ROOM
- ☐ COMFORT STATION
- ☐ OTHER: _____
- ☐ JOHN
- ☐ CAN
- ☐ HEAD
- ☐ POTTY
- ☐ CRAPPER
- ☐ WC

_____

RATINGS: 1 2 3 4 5
CLEANLINESS   ☆ ☆ ☆ ☆ ☆
AMBIENCE   ☆ ☆ ☆ ☆ ☆
AMENITIES   ☆ ☆ ☆ ☆ ☆
SOUND PROOFING   ☆ ☆ ☆ ☆ ☆
QUALITY OF THE FLUSH ☆ ☆ ☆ ☆ ☆
TOILET PAPER   ☆ ☆ ☆ ☆ ☆

OVERALL EXPERIENCE:
- ☐ BEST SEAT IN THE HOUSE ★ ★ ★ ★ ★
- ☐ WOULD POOP HERE AGAIN ★ ★ ★ ★
- ☐ SHIT GOT REAL ★ ★ ★
- ☐ SAME SHIT DIFFERENT HOUSE ★ ★
- ☐ THINGS JUST DIDN'T COME OUT RIGHT ★

THOUGHTS/MESSAGES: _____
_____
_____

Welcome! PLEASE SEAT YOURSELF AND ENJOY YOUR VISIT!

NAME: _____ DATE: _____ TIME: _____ DURATION OF VISIT: _____

HRS   MIN   SEC

PURPOSE FOR VISIT: ▢ #1 ▢ #2 ▢ OTHER: _____ SUCCESS? ▢ YES ▢ NO

FAVORITE EUPHEMISM FOR PERFORMING #1:

FAVORITE RESTROOM GRAFFITI OR YOUR ORIGNAL DOODLE:

FAVORITE EUPHEMISM FOR PERFORMING #2:

WHILE YOU WERE HERE, DID YOU:
- ▢ TEXT SOMEONE
- ▢ MAKE A PHONE CALL
- ▢ EMAIL
- ▢ CHECK SOCIAL MEDIA
- ▢ TAKE A SELFIE
- ▢ LOOK IN THE MEDICINE CABINET
- ▢ CHECK YOUR TEETH
- ▢ CHECK OUT YOUR BUTT
- ▢ CHECK YOUR FLY
- ▢ READ
- ▢ FIX YOUR HAIR
- ▢ TAKE SOME EXTRA "ME TIME"
- ▢ TALK TO YOURSELF
- ▢ CONDUCT BUSINESS OTHER THAN YOUR "BUSINESS." CARE TO SHARE?

FAVORITE NAME FOR THIS ROOM:
- ▢ BATHROOM
- ▢ TOILET
- ▢ POWDER ROOM
- ▢ LAVATORY
- ▢ SHITTER
- ▢ LOO
- ▢ LITTLE GIRLS ROOM
- ▢ LITTLE BOYS ROOM
- ▢ COMFORT STATION
- ▢ OTHER: _____
- ▢ JOHN
- ▢ CAN
- ▢ HEAD
- ▢ POTTY
- ▢ CRAPPER
- ▢ WC

RATINGS:
	1	2	3	4	5
CLEANLINESS	☆	☆	☆	☆	☆
AMBIENCE	☆	☆	☆	☆	☆
AMENITIES	☆	☆	☆	☆	☆
SOUND PROOFING	☆	☆	☆	☆	☆
QUALITY OF THE FLUSH	☆	☆	☆	☆	☆
TOILET PAPER	☆	☆	☆	☆	☆

OVERALL EXPERIENCE:
- ▢ BEST SEAT IN THE HOUSE ★ ★ ★ ★ ★
- ▢ WOULD POOP HERE AGAIN ★ ★ ★ ★
- ▢ SHIT GOT REAL ★ ★ ★
- ▢ SAME SHIT DIFFERENT HOUSE ★ ★
- ▢ THINGS JUST DIDN'T COME OUT RIGHT ★

THOUGHTS/MESSAGES: _____
_____
_____

Welcome! PLEASE SEAT YOURSELF AND ENJOY YOUR VISIT!

NAME: _____ DATE: _____ TIME: _____ DURATION OF VISIT: _____
HRS   MIN   SEC

PURPOSE FOR VISIT: 🧻 #1 🧻 #2 🧻 OTHER: _____ SUCCESS? 🧻 YES 🧻 NO

FAVORITE EUPHEMISM FOR PERFORMING #1:

FAVORITE EUPHEMISM FOR PERFORMING #2:

FAVORITE RESTROOM GRAFFITI OR YOUR ORIGNAL DOODLE:

WHILE YOU WERE HERE, DID YOU:
- ☐ TEXT SOMEONE
- ☐ MAKE A PHONE CALL
- ☐ EMAIL
- ☐ CHECK SOCIAL MEDIA
- ☐ TAKE A SELFIE
- ☐ LOOK IN THE MEDICINE CABINET
- ☐ CHECK YOUR TEETH
- ☐ CHECK OUT YOUR BUTT
- ☐ CHECK YOUR FLY
- ☐ READ
- ☐ FIX YOUR HAIR
- ☐ TAKE SOME EXTRA "ME TIME"
- ☐ TALK TO YOURSELF
- ☐ CONDUCT BUSINESS OTHER THAN YOUR "BUSINESS." CARE TO SHARE?
_____

FAVORITE NAME FOR THIS ROOM:
- ☐ BATHROOM
- ☐ TOILET
- ☐ POWDER ROOM
- ☐ LAVATORY
- ☐ SHITTER
- ☐ LOO
- ☐ LITTLE GIRLS ROOM
- ☐ LITTLE BOYS ROOM
- ☐ COMFORT STATION
- ☐ OTHER: _____
- ☐ JOHN
- ☐ CAN
- ☐ HEAD
- ☐ POTTY
- ☐ CRAPPER
- ☐ WC

_____

THOUGHTS/MESSAGES: _____
_____
_____

RATINGS: 1 2 3 4 5
CLEANLINESS   ☆ ☆ ☆ ☆ ☆
AMBIENCE   ☆ ☆ ☆ ☆ ☆
AMENITIES   ☆ ☆ ☆ ☆ ☆
SOUND PROOFING   ☆ ☆ ☆ ☆ ☆
QUALITY OF THE FLUSH   ☆ ☆ ☆ ☆ ☆
TOILET PAPER   ☆ ☆ ☆ ☆ ☆

OVERALL EXPERIENCE:
- ☐ BEST SEAT IN THE HOUSE ★ ★ ★ ★ ★
- ☐ WOULD POOP HERE AGAIN ★ ★ ★ ★
- ☐ SHIT GOT REAL ★ ★ ★
- ☐ SAME SHIT DIFFERENT HOUSE ★ ★
- ☐ THINGS JUST DIDN'T COME OUT RIGHT ★

Welcome! PLEASE SEAT YOURSELF AND ENJOY YOUR VISIT!

NAME: _____ DATE: _____ TIME: _____ DURATION OF VISIT: _____
HRS   MIN   SEC

PURPOSE FOR VISIT: ▢ #1 ▢ #2 ▢ OTHER: _____ SUCCESS? ▢ YES ▢ NO

FAVORITE EUPHEMISM FOR PERFORMING #1:

FAVORITE RESTROOM GRAFFITI OR YOUR ORIGNAL DOODLE:

FAVORITE EUPHEMISM FOR PERFORMING #2:

WHILE YOU WERE HERE, DID YOU:

- ▢ TEXT SOMEONE
- ▢ MAKE A PHONE CALL
- ▢ EMAIL
- ▢ CHECK SOCIAL MEDIA
- ▢ TAKE A SELFIE
- ▢ LOOK IN THE MEDICINE CABINET
- ▢ CHECK YOUR TEETH
- ▢ CHECK OUT YOUR BUTT
- ▢ CHECK YOUR FLY
- ▢ READ
- ▢ FIX YOUR HAIR
- ▢ TAKE SOME EXTRA "ME TIME"
- ▢ TALK TO YOURSELF
- ▢ CONDUCT BUSINESS OTHER THAN YOUR "BUSINESS." CARE TO SHARE?
  _____

FAVORITE NAME FOR THIS ROOM:

- ▢ BATHROOM
- ▢ TOILET
- ▢ POWDER ROOM
- ▢ LAVATORY
- ▢ SHITTER
- ▢ LOO
- ▢ LITTLE GIRLS ROOM
- ▢ LITTLE BOYS ROOM
- ▢ COMFORT STATION
- ▢ OTHER: _____
- ▢ JOHN
- ▢ CAN
- ▢ HEAD
- ▢ POTTY
- ▢ CRAPPER
- ▢ WC

_____
_____

THOUGHTS/MESSAGES: _____
_____
_____

RATINGS: 1 2 3 4 5

	1	2	3	4	5
CLEANLINESS	☆	☆	☆	☆	☆
AMBIENCE	☆	☆	☆	☆	☆
AMENITIES	☆	☆	☆	☆	☆
SOUND PROOFING	☆	☆	☆	☆	☆
QUALITY OF THE FLUSH	☆	☆	☆	☆	☆
TOILET PAPER	☆	☆	☆	☆	☆

OVERALL EXPERIENCE:

- ▢ BEST SEAT IN THE HOUSE ★ ★ ★ ★ ★
- ▢ WOULD POOP HERE AGAIN ★ ★ ★ ★
- ▢ SHIT GOT REAL ★ ★ ★
- ▢ SAME SHIT DIFFERENT HOUSE ★ ★
- ▢ THINGS JUST DIDN'T COME OUT RIGHT ★

Welcome! PLEASE SEAT YOURSELF AND ENJOY YOUR VISIT!

NAME: _____ DATE: _____ TIME: _____ DURATION OF VISIT: _____
                                                                              HRS   MIN   SEC

PURPOSE FOR VISIT: 🧻 #1   🧻 #2   🧻 OTHER: _____   SUCCESS? 🧻 YES   🧻 NO

FAVORITE EUPHEMISM FOR PERFORMING #1:

FAVORITE RESTROOM GRAFFITI OR YOUR ORIGNAL DOODLE:

FAVORITE EUPHEMISM FOR PERFORMING #2:

WHILE YOU WERE HERE, DID YOU:
- ☐ TEXT SOMEONE
- ☐ MAKE A PHONE CALL
- ☐ EMAIL
- ☐ CHECK SOCIAL MEDIA
- ☐ TAKE A SELFIE
- ☐ LOOK IN THE MEDICINE CABINET
- ☐ CHECK YOUR TEETH
- ☐ CHECK OUT YOUR BUTT
- ☐ CHECK YOUR FLY
- ☐ READ
- ☐ FIX YOUR HAIR
- ☐ TAKE SOME EXTRA "ME TIME"
- ☐ TALK TO YOURSELF
- ☐ CONDUCT BUSINESS OTHER THAN YOUR "BUSINESS." CARE TO SHARE?
  _____

FAVORITE NAME FOR THIS ROOM:
- ☐ BATHROOM
- ☐ TOILET
- ☐ POWDER ROOM
- ☐ LAVATORY
- ☐ SHITTER
- ☐ LOO
- ☐ LITTLE GIRLS ROOM
- ☐ LITTLE BOYS ROOM
- ☐ COMFORT STATION
- ☐ OTHER: _____
- ☐ JOHN
- ☐ CAN
- ☐ HEAD
- ☐ POTTY
- ☐ CRAPPER
- ☐ WC

_____

RATINGS: 1 2 3 4 5
CLEANLINESS   ☆ ☆ ☆ ☆ ☆
AMBIENCE   ☆ ☆ ☆ ☆ ☆
AMENITIES   ☆ ☆ ☆ ☆ ☆
SOUND PROOFING   ☆ ☆ ☆ ☆ ☆
QUALITY OF THE FLUSH   ☆ ☆ ☆ ☆ ☆
TOILET PAPER   ☆ ☆ ☆ ☆ ☆

OVERALL EXPERIENCE:
- ☐ BEST SEAT IN THE HOUSE   ★ ★ ★ ★ ★
- ☐ WOULD POOP HERE AGAIN   ★ ★ ★ ★
- ☐ SHIT GOT REAL   ★ ★ ★
- ☐ SAME SHIT DIFFERENT HOUSE   ★ ★
- ☐ THINGS JUST DIDN'T COME OUT RIGHT   ★

THOUGHTS/MESSAGES: _____
_____
_____

Welcome! PLEASE SEAT YOURSELF AND ENJOY YOUR VISIT!

NAME: _____ DATE: _____ TIME: _____ DURATION OF VISIT: _____
HRS   MIN   SEC

PURPOSE FOR VISIT: ▢ #1 ▢ #2 ▢ OTHER: _____ SUCCESS? ▢ YES ▢ NO

FAVORITE EUPHEMISM FOR PERFORMING #1:

FAVORITE RESTROOM GRAFFITI OR YOUR ORIGNAL DOODLE:

FAVORITE EUPHEMISM FOR PERFORMING #2:

WHILE YOU WERE HERE, DID YOU:
- ☐ TEXT SOMEONE
- ☐ MAKE A PHONE CALL
- ☐ EMAIL
- ☐ CHECK SOCIAL MEDIA
- ☐ TAKE A SELFIE
- ☐ LOOK IN THE MEDICINE CABINET
- ☐ CHECK YOUR TEETH
- ☐ CHECK OUT YOUR BUTT
- ☐ CHECK YOUR FLY
- ☐ READ
- ☐ FIX YOUR HAIR
- ☐ TAKE SOME EXTRA "ME TIME"
- ☐ TALK TO YOURSELF
- ☐ CONDUCT BUSINESS OTHER THAN YOUR "BUSINESS." CARE TO SHARE?

FAVORITE NAME FOR THIS ROOM:
- ☐ BATHROOM
- ☐ TOILET
- ☐ POWDER ROOM
- ☐ LAVATORY
- ☐ SHITTER
- ☐ LOO
- ☐ LITTLE GIRLS ROOM
- ☐ LITTLE BOYS ROOM
- ☐ COMFORT STATION
- ☐ OTHER: _____

- ☐ JOHN
- ☐ CAN
- ☐ HEAD
- ☐ POTTY
- ☐ CRAPPER
- ☐ WC

RATINGS: 1 2 3 4 5
	1	2	3	4	5
CLEANLINESS	☆	☆	☆	☆	☆
AMBIENCE	☆	☆	☆	☆	☆
AMENITIES	☆	☆	☆	☆	☆
SOUND PROOFING	☆	☆	☆	☆	☆
QUALITY OF THE FLUSH	☆	☆	☆	☆	☆
TOILET PAPER	☆	☆	☆	☆	☆

OVERALL EXPERIENCE:
- ☐ BEST SEAT IN THE HOUSE ★ ★ ★ ★ ★
- ☐ WOULD POOP HERE AGAIN ★ ★ ★ ★
- ☐ SHIT GOT REAL ★ ★ ★
- ☐ SAME SHIT DIFFERENT HOUSE ★ ★
- ☐ THINGS JUST DIDN'T COME OUT RIGHT ★

THOUGHTS/MESSAGES: _____
_____
_____

Welcome! PLEASE SEAT YOURSELF AND ENJOY YOUR VISIT!

NAME: _____ DATE: _____ TIME: _____ DURATION OF VISIT: _____
                                                                                  HRS   MIN   SEC

PURPOSE FOR VISIT: 🧻 #1 🧻 #2 🧻 OTHER: _____ SUCCESS? 🧻 YES 🧻 NO

FAVORITE EUPHEMISM FOR PERFORMING #1:

FAVORITE EUPHEMISM FOR PERFORMING #2:

FAVORITE RESTROOM GRAFFITI OR YOUR ORIGNAL DOODLE:

WHILE YOU WERE HERE, DID YOU:
- ☐ TEXT SOMEONE
- ☐ MAKE A PHONE CALL
- ☐ EMAIL
- ☐ CHECK SOCIAL MEDIA
- ☐ TAKE A SELFIE
- ☐ LOOK IN THE MEDICINE CABINET
- ☐ CHECK YOUR TEETH
- ☐ CHECK OUT YOUR BUTT
- ☐ CHECK YOUR FLY
- ☐ READ
- ☐ FIX YOUR HAIR
- ☐ TAKE SOME EXTRA "ME TIME"
- ☐ TALK TO YOURSELF
- ☐ CONDUCT BUSINESS OTHER THAN YOUR "BUSINESS." CARE TO SHARE?
  _____

FAVORITE NAME FOR THIS ROOM:
- ☐ BATHROOM
- ☐ TOILET
- ☐ POWDER ROOM
- ☐ LAVATORY
- ☐ SHITTER
- ☐ LOO
- ☐ LITTLE GIRLS ROOM
- ☐ LITTLE BOYS ROOM
- ☐ COMFORT STATION
- ☐ OTHER: _____
- ☐ JOHN
- ☐ CAN
- ☐ HEAD
- ☐ POTTY
- ☐ CRAPPER
- ☐ WC

_____

RATINGS:

	1	2	3	4	5
CLEANLINESS	☆	☆	☆	☆	☆
AMBIENCE	☆	☆	☆	☆	☆
AMENITIES	☆	☆	☆	☆	☆
SOUND PROOFING	☆	☆	☆	☆	☆
QUALITY OF THE FLUSH	☆	☆	☆	☆	☆
TOILET PAPER	☆	☆	☆	☆	☆

OVERALL EXPERIENCE:
- ☐ BEST SEAT IN THE HOUSE ★ ★ ★ ★ ★
- ☐ WOULD POOP HERE AGAIN ★ ★ ★ ★
- ☐ SHIT GOT REAL ★ ★ ★
- ☐ SAME SHIT DIFFERENT HOUSE ★ ★
- ☐ THINGS JUST DIDN'T COME OUT RIGHT ★

THOUGHTS/MESSAGES: _____
_____
_____

Welcome! PLEASE SEAT YOURSELF AND ENJOY YOUR VISIT!

NAME: _____ DATE: _____ TIME: _____ DURATION OF VISIT: _____
HRS   MIN   SEC

PURPOSE FOR VISIT: ☐ #1 ☐ #2 ☐ OTHER: _____ SUCCESS? ☐ YES ☐ NO

FAVORITE EUPHEMISM FOR PERFORMING #1:

FAVORITE RESTROOM GRAFFITI OR YOUR ORIGNAL DOODLE:

FAVORITE EUPHEMISM FOR PERFORMING #2:

WHILE YOU WERE HERE, DID YOU:
☐ TEXT SOMEONE
☐ MAKE A PHONE CALL
☐ EMAIL
☐ CHECK SOCIAL MEDIA
☐ TAKE A SELFIE
☐ LOOK IN THE MEDICINE CABINET
☐ CHECK YOUR TEETH
☐ CHECK OUT YOUR BUTT
☐ CHECK YOUR FLY
☐ READ
☐ FIX YOUR HAIR
☐ TAKE SOME EXTRA "ME TIME"
☐ TALK TO YOURSELF
☐ CONDUCT BUSINESS OTHER THAN YOUR "BUSINESS." CARE TO SHARE?

FAVORITE NAME FOR THIS ROOM:
☐ BATHROOM   ☐ JOHN
☐ TOILET   ☐ CAN
☐ POWDER ROOM   ☐ HEAD
☐ LAVATORY   ☐ POTTY
☐ SHITTER   ☐ CRAPPER
☐ LOO   ☐ WC
☐ LITTLE GIRLS ROOM
☐ LITTLE BOYS ROOM
☐ COMFORT STATION
☐ OTHER: _____

RATINGS: 1 2 3 4 5
CLEANLINESS   ☆ ☆ ☆ ☆ ☆
AMBIENCE   ☆ ☆ ☆ ☆ ☆
AMENITIES   ☆ ☆ ☆ ☆ ☆
SOUND PROOFING   ☆ ☆ ☆ ☆ ☆
QUALITY OF THE FLUSH ☆ ☆ ☆ ☆ ☆
TOILET PAPER   ☆ ☆ ☆ ☆ ☆

OVERALL EXPERIENCE:
☐ BEST SEAT IN THE HOUSE   ★ ★ ★ ★ ★
☐ WOULD POOP HERE AGAIN   ★ ★ ★ ★
☐ SHIT GOT REAL   ★ ★ ★
☐ SAME SHIT DIFFERENT HOUSE   ★ ★
☐ THINGS JUST DIDN'T COME OUT RIGHT ★

THOUGHTS/MESSAGES: _____
_____
_____

Welcome! PLEASE SEAT YOURSELF AND ENJOY YOUR VISIT!

NAME: _____ DATE: _____ TIME: _____ DURATION OF VISIT: _____
HRS   MIN   SEC

PURPOSE FOR VISIT: [ ] #1 [ ] #2 [ ] OTHER: _____ SUCCESS? [ ] YES [ ] NO

FAVORITE EUPHEMISM FOR PERFORMING #1:

FAVORITE EUPHEMISM FOR PERFORMING #2:

FAVORITE RESTROOM GRAFFITI OR YOUR ORIGNAL DOODLE:

WHILE YOU WERE HERE, DID YOU:
- ☐ TEXT SOMEONE
- ☐ MAKE A PHONE CALL
- ☐ EMAIL
- ☐ CHECK SOCIAL MEDIA
- ☐ TAKE A SELFIE
- ☐ LOOK IN THE MEDICINE CABINET
- ☐ CHECK YOUR TEETH
- ☐ CHECK OUT YOUR BUTT
- ☐ CHECK YOUR FLY
- ☐ READ
- ☐ FIX YOUR HAIR
- ☐ TAKE SOME EXTRA "ME TIME"
- ☐ TALK TO YOURSELF
- ☐ CONDUCT BUSINESS OTHER THAN YOUR "BUSINESS." CARE TO SHARE?

FAVORITE NAME FOR THIS ROOM:
- ☐ BATHROOM
- ☐ TOILET
- ☐ POWDER ROOM
- ☐ LAVATORY
- ☐ SHITTER
- ☐ LOO
- ☐ LITTLE GIRLS ROOM
- ☐ LITTLE BOYS ROOM
- ☐ COMFORT STATION
- ☐ OTHER: _____
- ☐ JOHN
- ☐ CAN
- ☐ HEAD
- ☐ POTTY
- ☐ CRAPPER
- ☐ WC

RATINGS:
	1	2	3	4	5
CLEANLINESS	☆	☆	☆	☆	☆
AMBIENCE	☆	☆	☆	☆	☆
AMENITIES	☆	☆	☆	☆	☆
SOUND PROOFING	☆	☆	☆	☆	☆
QUALITY OF THE FLUSH	☆	☆	☆	☆	☆
TOILET PAPER	☆	☆	☆	☆	☆

OVERALL EXPERIENCE:
- ☐ BEST SEAT IN THE HOUSE ★ ★ ★ ★ ★
- ☐ WOULD POOP HERE AGAIN ★ ★ ★ ★
- ☐ SHIT GOT REAL ★ ★ ★
- ☐ SAME SHIT DIFFERENT HOUSE ★ ★
- ☐ THINGS JUST DIDN'T COME OUT RIGHT ★

THOUGHTS/MESSAGES: _____

Welcome! PLEASE SEAT YOURSELF AND ENJOY YOUR VISIT!

NAME: _____ DATE: _____ TIME: _____ DURATION OF VISIT: _____
HRS MIN SEC

PURPOSE FOR VISIT: ▢ #1 ▢ #2 ▢ OTHER: _____ SUCCESS? ▢ YES ▢ NO

FAVORITE EUPHEMISM FOR PERFORMING #1:

FAVORITE EUPHEMISM FOR PERFORMING #2:

FAVORITE RESTROOM GRAFFITI OR YOUR ORIGNAL DOODLE:

WHILE YOU WERE HERE, DID YOU:
☐ TEXT SOMEONE
☐ MAKE A PHONE CALL
☐ EMAIL
☐ CHECK SOCIAL MEDIA
☐ TAKE A SELFIE
☐ LOOK IN THE MEDICINE CABINET
☐ CHECK YOUR TEETH
☐ CHECK OUT YOUR BUTT
☐ CHECK YOUR FLY
☐ READ
☐ FIX YOUR HAIR
☐ TAKE SOME EXTRA "ME TIME"
☐ TALK TO YOURSELF
☐ CONDUCT BUSINESS OTHER THAN YOUR "BUSINESS." CARE TO SHARE?

FAVORITE NAME FOR THIS ROOM:
☐ BATHROOM   ☐ JOHN
☐ TOILET   ☐ CAN
☐ POWDER ROOM   ☐ HEAD
☐ LAVATORY   ☐ POTTY
☐ SHITTER   ☐ CRAPPER
☐ LOO   ☐ WC
☐ LITTLE GIRLS ROOM
☐ LITTLE BOYS ROOM
☐ COMFORT STATION
☐ OTHER: _____

RATINGS:
	1	2	3	4	5
CLEANLINESS	☆	☆	☆	☆	☆
AMBIENCE	☆	☆	☆	☆	☆
AMENITIES	☆	☆	☆	☆	☆
SOUND PROOFING	☆	☆	☆	☆	☆
QUALITY OF THE FLUSH	☆	☆	☆	☆	☆
TOILET PAPER	☆	☆	☆	☆	☆

OVERALL EXPERIENCE:
☐ BEST SEAT IN THE HOUSE ★ ★ ★ ★ ★
☐ WOULD POOP HERE AGAIN ★ ★ ★ ★
☐ SHIT GOT REAL ★ ★ ★
☐ SAME SHIT DIFFERENT HOUSE ★ ★
☐ THINGS JUST DIDN'T COME OUT RIGHT ★

THOUGHTS/MESSAGES: _____
_____
_____

Welcome! PLEASE SEAT YOURSELF AND ENJOY YOUR VISIT!

NAME: _____ DATE: _____ TIME: _____ DURATION OF VISIT: _____
HRS   MIN   SEC

PURPOSE FOR VISIT: ▢ #1 ▢ #2 ▢ OTHER: _____ SUCCESS? ▢ YES ▢ NO

FAVORITE EUPHEMISM FOR PERFORMING #1:

FAVORITE RESTROOM GRAFFITI OR YOUR ORIGNAL DOODLE:

FAVORITE EUPHEMISM FOR PERFORMING #2:

WHILE YOU WERE HERE, DID YOU:
- ☐ TEXT SOMEONE
- ☐ MAKE A PHONE CALL
- ☐ EMAIL
- ☐ CHECK SOCIAL MEDIA
- ☐ TAKE A SELFIE
- ☐ LOOK IN THE MEDICINE CABINET
- ☐ CHECK YOUR TEETH
- ☐ CHECK OUT YOUR BUTT
- ☐ CHECK YOUR FLY
- ☐ READ
- ☐ FIX YOUR HAIR
- ☐ TAKE SOME EXTRA "ME TIME"
- ☐ TALK TO YOURSELF
- ☐ CONDUCT BUSINESS OTHER THAN YOUR "BUSINESS." CARE TO SHARE?
_____

FAVORITE NAME FOR THIS ROOM:
- ☐ BATHROOM
- ☐ TOILET
- ☐ POWDER ROOM
- ☐ LAVATORY
- ☐ SHITTER
- ☐ LOO
- ☐ LITTLE GIRLS ROOM
- ☐ LITTLE BOYS ROOM
- ☐ COMFORT STATION
- ☐ OTHER: _____
- ☐ JOHN
- ☐ CAN
- ☐ HEAD
- ☐ POTTY
- ☐ CRAPPER
- ☐ WC

_____

THOUGHTS/MESSAGES: _____
_____
_____

RATINGS: 1 2 3 4 5
CLEANLINESS   ☆ ☆ ☆ ☆ ☆
AMBIENCE   ☆ ☆ ☆ ☆ ☆
AMENITIES   ☆ ☆ ☆ ☆ ☆
SOUND PROOFING   ☆ ☆ ☆ ☆ ☆
QUALITY OF THE FLUSH ☆ ☆ ☆ ☆ ☆
TOILET PAPER   ☆ ☆ ☆ ☆ ☆

OVERALL EXPERIENCE:
- ☐ BEST SEAT IN THE HOUSE   ★ ★ ★ ★ ★
- ☐ WOULD POOP HERE AGAIN   ★ ★ ★ ★
- ☐ SHIT GOT REAL   ★ ★ ★
- ☐ SAME SHIT DIFFERENT HOUSE   ★ ★
- ☐ THINGS JUST DIDN'T COME OUT RIGHT ★

Welcome! PLEASE SEAT YOURSELF AND ENJOY YOUR VISIT!

NAME: _____ DATE: _____ TIME: _____ DURATION OF VISIT: _____
HRS   MIN   SEC

PURPOSE FOR VISIT: ☐ #1 ☐ #2 ☐ OTHER: _____ SUCCESS? ☐ YES ☐ NO

FAVORITE EUPHEMISM FOR PERFORMING #1:

FAVORITE RESTROOM GRAFFITI OR YOUR ORIGNAL DOODLE:

FAVORITE EUPHEMISM FOR PERFORMING #2:

WHILE YOU WERE HERE, DID YOU:
☐ TEXT SOMEONE
☐ MAKE A PHONE CALL
☐ EMAIL
☐ CHECK SOCIAL MEDIA
☐ TAKE A SELFIE
☐ LOOK IN THE MEDICINE CABINET
☐ CHECK YOUR TEETH
☐ CHECK OUT YOUR BUTT
☐ CHECK YOUR FLY
☐ READ
☐ FIX YOUR HAIR
☐ TAKE SOME EXTRA "ME TIME"
☐ TALK TO YOURSELF
☐ CONDUCT BUSINESS OTHER THAN YOUR "BUSINESS." CARE TO SHARE?
_____

FAVORITE NAME FOR THIS ROOM:
☐ BATHROOM   ☐ JOHN
☐ TOILET   ☐ CAN
☐ POWDER ROOM   ☐ HEAD
☐ LAVATORY   ☐ POTTY
☐ SHITTER   ☐ CRAPPER
☐ LOO   ☐ WC
☐ LITTLE GIRLS ROOM
☐ LITTLE BOYS ROOM
☐ COMFORT STATION
☐ OTHER: _____
_____

RATINGS:
	1	2	3	4	5
CLEANLINESS	☆	☆	☆	☆	☆
AMBIENCE	☆	☆	☆	☆	☆
AMENITIES	☆	☆	☆	☆	☆
SOUND PROOFING	☆	☆	☆	☆	☆
QUALITY OF THE FLUSH	☆	☆	☆	☆	☆
TOILET PAPER	☆	☆	☆	☆	☆

OVERALL EXPERIENCE:
☐ BEST SEAT IN THE HOUSE   ★ ★ ★ ★ ★
☐ WOULD POOP HERE AGAIN   ★ ★ ★ ★
☐ SHIT GOT REAL   ★ ★ ★
☐ SAME SHIT DIFFERENT HOUSE ★ ★
☐ THINGS JUST DIDN'T COME OUT RIGHT ★

THOUGHTS/MESSAGES: _____
_____
_____

Welcome! PLEASE SEAT YOURSELF AND ENJOY YOUR VISIT!

NAME: _____ DATE: _____ TIME: _____ **DURATION OF VISIT:** _____
HRS   MIN   SEC

PURPOSE FOR VISIT: ☐ #1   ☐ #2   ☐ OTHER: _____   **SUCCESS?** ☐ YES ☐ NO

FAVORITE EUPHEMISM FOR PERFORMING #1:

FAVORITE RESTROOM GRAFFITI OR YOUR ORIGNAL DOODLE:

FAVORITE EUPHEMISM FOR PERFORMING #2:

WHILE YOU WERE HERE, DID YOU:
☐ TEXT SOMEONE
☐ MAKE A PHONE CALL
☐ EMAIL
☐ CHECK SOCIAL MEDIA
☐ TAKE A SELFIE
☐ LOOK IN THE MEDICINE CABINET
☐ CHECK YOUR TEETH
☐ CHECK OUT YOUR BUTT
☐ CHECK YOUR FLY
☐ READ
☐ FIX YOUR HAIR
☐ TAKE SOME EXTRA "ME TIME"
☐ TALK TO YOURSELF
☐ CONDUCT BUSINESS OTHER THAN YOUR "BUSINESS." CARE TO SHARE?
_____

FAVORITE NAME FOR THIS ROOM:
☐ BATHROOM   ☐ JOHN
☐ TOILET   ☐ CAN
☐ POWDER ROOM   ☐ HEAD
☐ LAVATORY   ☐ POTTY
☐ SHITTER   ☐ CRAPPER
☐ LOO   ☐ WC
☐ LITTLE GIRLS ROOM
☐ LITTLE BOYS ROOM
☐ COMFORT STATION
☐ OTHER: _____
_____

THOUGHTS/MESSAGES: _____
_____
_____

RATINGS: 1 2 3 4 5
CLEANLINESS   ☆ ☆ ☆ ☆ ☆
AMBIENCE   ☆ ☆ ☆ ☆ ☆
AMENITIES   ☆ ☆ ☆ ☆ ☆
SOUND PROOFING   ☆ ☆ ☆ ☆ ☆
QUALITY OF THE FLUSH ☆ ☆ ☆ ☆ ☆
TOILET PAPER   ☆ ☆ ☆ ☆ ☆

OVERALL EXPERIENCE:
☐ BEST SEAT IN THE HOUSE ★ ★ ★ ★ ★
☐ WOULD POOP HERE AGAIN ★ ★ ★ ★
☐ SHIT GOT REAL ★ ★ ★
☐ SAME SHIT DIFFERENT HOUSE ★ ★
☐ THINGS JUST DIDN'T COME OUT RIGHT ★

Welcome! PLEASE SEAT YOURSELF AND ENJOY YOUR VISIT!

NAME: _____ DATE: _____ TIME: _____ DURATION OF VISIT: _____
HRS   MIN   SEC

PURPOSE FOR VISIT: ☐ #1   ☐ #2   ☐ OTHER: _____   SUCCESS? ☐ YES ☐ NO

FAVORITE EUPHEMISM FOR PERFORMING #1:

FAVORITE RESTROOM GRAFFITI OR YOUR ORIGNAL DOODLE:

FAVORITE EUPHEMISM FOR PERFORMING #2:

WHILE YOU WERE HERE, DID YOU:
☐ TEXT SOMEONE
☐ MAKE A PHONE CALL
☐ EMAIL
☐ CHECK SOCIAL MEDIA
☐ TAKE A SELFIE
☐ LOOK IN THE MEDICINE CABINET
☐ CHECK YOUR TEETH
☐ CHECK OUT YOUR BUTT
☐ CHECK YOUR FLY
☐ READ
☐ FIX YOUR HAIR
☐ TAKE SOME EXTRA "ME TIME"
☐ TALK TO YOURSELF
☐ CONDUCT BUSINESS OTHER THAN YOUR "BUSINESS." CARE TO SHARE?

FAVORITE NAME FOR THIS ROOM:
☐ BATHROOM   ☐ JOHN
☐ TOILET   ☐ CAN
☐ POWDER ROOM   ☐ HEAD
☐ LAVATORY   ☐ POTTY
☐ SHITTER   ☐ CRAPPER
☐ LOO   ☐ WC
☐ LITTLE GIRLS ROOM
☐ LITTLE BOYS ROOM
☐ COMFORT STATION
☐ OTHER: _____

THOUGHTS/MESSAGES: _____
_____
_____

RATINGS: 1 2 3 4 5
CLEANLINESS   ☆ ☆ ☆ ☆ ☆
AMBIENCE   ☆ ☆ ☆ ☆ ☆
AMENITIES   ☆ ☆ ☆ ☆ ☆
SOUND PROOFING   ☆ ☆ ☆ ☆ ☆
QUALITY OF THE FLUSH ☆ ☆ ☆ ☆ ☆
TOILET PAPER   ☆ ☆ ☆ ☆ ☆

OVERALL EXPERIENCE:
☐ BEST SEAT IN THE HOUSE   ★ ★ ★ ★ ★
☐ WOULD POOP HERE AGAIN   ★ ★ ★ ★
☐ SHIT GOT REAL   ★ ★ ★
☐ SAME SHIT DIFFERENT HOUSE   ★ ★
☐ THINGS JUST DIDN'T COME OUT RIGHT ★

 **PLEASE SEAT YOURSELF AND ENJOY YOUR VISIT!**

NAME: _____	DATE: _____	TIME: _____	DURATION OF VISIT: _____

HRS   MIN   SEC

PURPOSE FOR VISIT: 🧻 #1   🧻 #2   🧻 OTHER: _____   SUCCESS? 🧻 YES 🧻 NO

FAVORITE EUPHEMISM FOR PERFORMING #1:

FAVORITE RESTROOM GRAFFITI OR YOUR ORIGNAL DOODLE:

FAVORITE EUPHEMISM FOR PERFORMING #2:

WHILE YOU WERE HERE, DID YOU:
- ☐ TEXT SOMEONE
- ☐ MAKE A PHONE CALL
- ☐ EMAIL
- ☐ CHECK SOCIAL MEDIA
- ☐ TAKE A SELFIE
- ☐ LOOK IN THE MEDICINE CABINET
- ☐ CHECK YOUR TEETH
- ☐ CHECK OUT YOUR BUTT
- ☐ CHECK YOUR FLY
- ☐ READ
- ☐ FIX YOUR HAIR
- ☐ TAKE SOME EXTRA "ME TIME"
- ☐ TALK TO YOURSELF
- ☐ CONDUCT BUSINESS OTHER THAN YOUR "BUSINESS." CARE TO SHARE?
  _____

FAVORITE NAME FOR THIS ROOM:
- ☐ BATHROOM
- ☐ TOILET
- ☐ POWDER ROOM
- ☐ LAVATORY
- ☐ SHITTER
- ☐ LOO
- ☐ LITTLE GIRLS ROOM
- ☐ LITTLE BOYS ROOM
- ☐ COMFORT STATION
- ☐ OTHER: _____
- ☐ JOHN
- ☐ CAN
- ☐ HEAD
- ☐ POTTY
- ☐ CRAPPER
- ☐ WC

_____

RATINGS:

	1	2	3	4	5
CLEANLINESS	☆	☆	☆	☆	☆
AMBIENCE	☆	☆	☆	☆	☆
AMENITIES	☆	☆	☆	☆	☆
SOUND PROOFING	☆	☆	☆	☆	☆
QUALITY OF THE FLUSH	☆	☆	☆	☆	☆
TOILET PAPER	☆	☆	☆	☆	☆

OVERALL EXPERIENCE:
- ☐ BEST SEAT IN THE HOUSE ★ ★ ★ ★ ★
- ☐ WOULD POOP HERE AGAIN ★ ★ ★ ★
- ☐ SHIT GOT REAL ★ ★ ★
- ☐ SAME SHIT DIFFERENT HOUSE ★ ★
- ☐ THINGS JUST DIDN'T COME OUT RIGHT ★

THOUGHTS/MESSAGES: _____

_____

_____

Welcome! PLEASE SEAT YOURSELF AND ENJOY YOUR VISIT!

NAME: _____ DATE: _____ TIME: _____ DURATION OF VISIT: _____

HRS   MIN   SEC

PURPOSE FOR VISIT: ☐ #1 ☐ #2 ☐ OTHER: _____ SUCCESS? ☐ YES ☐ NO

FAVORITE EUPHEMISM FOR PERFORMING #1:

FAVORITE RESTROOM GRAFFITI OR YOUR ORIGNAL DOODLE:

FAVORITE EUPHEMISM FOR PERFORMING #2:

WHILE YOU WERE HERE, DID YOU:
- ☐ TEXT SOMEONE
- ☐ MAKE A PHONE CALL
- ☐ EMAIL
- ☐ CHECK SOCIAL MEDIA
- ☐ TAKE A SELFIE
- ☐ LOOK IN THE MEDICINE CABINET
- ☐ CHECK YOUR TEETH
- ☐ CHECK OUT YOUR BUTT
- ☐ CHECK YOUR FLY
- ☐ READ
- ☐ FIX YOUR HAIR
- ☐ TAKE SOME EXTRA "ME TIME"
- ☐ TALK TO YOURSELF
- ☐ CONDUCT BUSINESS OTHER THAN YOUR "BUSINESS." CARE TO SHARE?
_____

FAVORITE NAME FOR THIS ROOM:
- ☐ BATHROOM
- ☐ TOILET
- ☐ POWDER ROOM
- ☐ LAVATORY
- ☐ SHITTER
- ☐ LOO
- ☐ LITTLE GIRLS ROOM
- ☐ LITTLE BOYS ROOM
- ☐ COMFORT STATION
- ☐ OTHER: _____

- ☐ JOHN
- ☐ CAN
- ☐ HEAD
- ☐ POTTY
- ☐ CRAPPER
- ☐ WC

_____
_____

RATINGS:
	1	2	3	4	5
CLEANLINESS	☆	☆	☆	☆	☆
AMBIENCE	☆	☆	☆	☆	☆
AMENITIES	☆	☆	☆	☆	☆
SOUND PROOFING	☆	☆	☆	☆	☆
QUALITY OF THE FLUSH	☆	☆	☆	☆	☆
TOILET PAPER	☆	☆	☆	☆	☆

OVERALL EXPERIENCE:
- ☐ BEST SEAT IN THE HOUSE ★ ★ ★ ★ ★
- ☐ WOULD POOP HERE AGAIN ★ ★ ★ ★
- ☐ SHIT GOT REAL ★ ★ ★
- ☐ SAME SHIT DIFFERENT HOUSE ★ ★
- ☐ THINGS JUST DIDN'T COME OUT RIGHT ★

THOUGHTS/MESSAGES: _____
_____
_____

Welcome! PLEASE SEAT YOURSELF AND ENJOY YOUR VISIT!

NAME: _____ DATE: _____ TIME: _____ DURATION OF VISIT: _____
HRS MIN SEC

PURPOSE FOR VISIT: 🧻 #1 🧻 #2 🧻 OTHER: _____ SUCCESS? 🧻 YES 🧻 NO

FAVORITE EUPHEMISM FOR PERFORMING #1:

FAVORITE RESTROOM GRAFFITI OR YOUR ORIGNAL DOODLE:

FAVORITE EUPHEMISM FOR PERFORMING #2:

WHILE YOU WERE HERE, DID YOU:
- ☐ TEXT SOMEONE
- ☐ MAKE A PHONE CALL
- ☐ EMAIL
- ☐ CHECK SOCIAL MEDIA
- ☐ TAKE A SELFIE
- ☐ LOOK IN THE MEDICINE CABINET
- ☐ CHECK YOUR TEETH
- ☐ CHECK OUT YOUR BUTT
- ☐ CHECK YOUR FLY
- ☐ READ
- ☐ FIX YOUR HAIR
- ☐ TAKE SOME EXTRA "ME TIME"
- ☐ TALK TO YOURSELF
- ☐ CONDUCT BUSINESS OTHER THAN YOUR "BUSINESS." CARE TO SHARE?

FAVORITE NAME FOR THIS ROOM:
- ☐ BATHROOM
- ☐ TOILET
- ☐ POWDER ROOM
- ☐ LAVATORY
- ☐ SHITTER
- ☐ LOO
- ☐ LITTLE GIRLS ROOM
- ☐ LITTLE BOYS ROOM
- ☐ COMFORT STATION
- ☐ OTHER: _____
- ☐ JOHN
- ☐ CAN
- ☐ HEAD
- ☐ POTTY
- ☐ CRAPPER
- ☐ WC

RATINGS:
	1	2	3	4	5
CLEANLINESS	☆	☆	☆	☆	☆
AMBIENCE	☆	☆	☆	☆	☆
AMENITIES	☆	☆	☆	☆	☆
SOUND PROOFING	☆	☆	☆	☆	☆
QUALITY OF THE FLUSH	☆	☆	☆	☆	☆
TOILET PAPER	☆	☆	☆	☆	☆

OVERALL EXPERIENCE:
- ☐ BEST SEAT IN THE HOUSE ★ ★ ★ ★ ★
- ☐ WOULD POOP HERE AGAIN ★ ★ ★ ★
- ☐ SHIT GOT REAL ★ ★ ★
- ☐ SAME SHIT DIFFERENT HOUSE ★ ★
- ☐ THINGS JUST DIDN'T COME OUT RIGHT ★

THOUGHTS/MESSAGES: _____

Welcome! PLEASE SEAT YOURSELF AND ENJOY YOUR VISIT!

NAME: _____ DATE: _____ TIME: _____ DURATION OF VISIT: _____

HRS   MIN   SEC

PURPOSE FOR VISIT: ☐ #1 ☐ #2 ☐ OTHER: _____ SUCCESS? ☐ YES ☐ NO

FAVORITE EUPHEMISM FOR PERFORMING #1:

FAVORITE RESTROOM GRAFFITI OR YOUR ORIGNAL DOODLE:

FAVORITE EUPHEMISM FOR PERFORMING #2:

WHILE YOU WERE HERE, DID YOU:
☐ TEXT SOMEONE
☐ MAKE A PHONE CALL
☐ EMAIL
☐ CHECK SOCIAL MEDIA
☐ TAKE A SELFIE
☐ LOOK IN THE MEDICINE CABINET
☐ CHECK YOUR TEETH
☐ CHECK OUT YOUR BUTT
☐ CHECK YOUR FLY
☐ READ
☐ FIX YOUR HAIR
☐ TAKE SOME EXTRA "ME TIME"
☐ TALK TO YOURSELF
☐ CONDUCT BUSINESS OTHER THAN YOUR "BUSINESS." CARE TO SHARE?

FAVORITE NAME FOR THIS ROOM:
☐ BATHROOM   ☐ JOHN
☐ TOILET   ☐ CAN
☐ POWDER ROOM   ☐ HEAD
☐ LAVATORY   ☐ POTTY
☐ SHITTER   ☐ CRAPPER
☐ LOO   ☐ WC
☐ LITTLE GIRLS ROOM
☐ LITTLE BOYS ROOM
☐ COMFORT STATION
☐ OTHER: _____

RATINGS:
	1 2 3 4 5
CLEANLINESS	☆ ☆ ☆ ☆ ☆
AMBIENCE	☆ ☆ ☆ ☆ ☆
AMENITIES	☆ ☆ ☆ ☆ ☆
SOUND PROOFING	☆ ☆ ☆ ☆ ☆
QUALITY OF THE FLUSH	☆ ☆ ☆ ☆ ☆
TOILET PAPER	☆ ☆ ☆ ☆ ☆

OVERALL EXPERIENCE:
☐ BEST SEAT IN THE HOUSE ★ ★ ★ ★ ★
☐ WOULD POOP HERE AGAIN ★ ★ ★ ★
☐ SHIT GOT REAL ★ ★ ★
☐ SAME SHIT DIFFERENT HOUSE ★ ★
☐ THINGS JUST DIDN'T COME OUT RIGHT ★

THOUGHTS/MESSAGES: _____

Welcome! PLEASE SEAT YOURSELF AND ENJOY YOUR VISIT!

NAME: _____ DATE: _____ TIME: _____ DURATION OF VISIT: _____
HRS   MIN   SEC

PURPOSE FOR VISIT: ▯ #1 ▯ #2 ▯ OTHER: _____ SUCCESS? ▯ YES ▯ NO

FAVORITE EUPHEMISM FOR PERFORMING #1:

FAVORITE RESTROOM GRAFFITI OR YOUR ORIGNAL DOODLE:

FAVORITE EUPHEMISM FOR PERFORMING #2:

WHILE YOU WERE HERE, DID YOU:
- ☐ TEXT SOMEONE
- ☐ MAKE A PHONE CALL
- ☐ EMAIL
- ☐ CHECK SOCIAL MEDIA
- ☐ TAKE A SELFIE
- ☐ LOOK IN THE MEDICINE CABINET
- ☐ CHECK YOUR TEETH
- ☐ CHECK OUT YOUR BUTT
- ☐ CHECK YOUR FLY
- ☐ READ
- ☐ FIX YOUR HAIR
- ☐ TAKE SOME EXTRA "ME TIME"
- ☐ TALK TO YOURSELF
- ☐ CONDUCT BUSINESS OTHER THAN YOUR "BUSINESS." CARE TO SHARE?
_____

FAVORITE NAME FOR THIS ROOM:
- ☐ BATHROOM
- ☐ TOILET
- ☐ POWDER ROOM
- ☐ LAVATORY
- ☐ SHITTER
- ☐ LOO
- ☐ LITTLE GIRLS ROOM
- ☐ LITTLE BOYS ROOM
- ☐ COMFORT STATION
- ☐ OTHER: _____
- ☐ JOHN
- ☐ CAN
- ☐ HEAD
- ☐ POTTY
- ☐ CRAPPER
- ☐ WC

_____

THOUGHTS/MESSAGES: _____
_____
_____

RATINGS: 1 2 3 4 5
CLEANLINESS   ☆ ☆ ☆ ☆ ☆
AMBIENCE   ☆ ☆ ☆ ☆ ☆
AMENITIES   ☆ ☆ ☆ ☆ ☆
SOUND PROOFING   ☆ ☆ ☆ ☆ ☆
QUALITY OF THE FLUSH ☆ ☆ ☆ ☆ ☆
TOILET PAPER   ☆ ☆ ☆ ☆ ☆

OVERALL EXPERIENCE:
- ☐ BEST SEAT IN THE HOUSE   ★ ★ ★ ★ ★
- ☐ WOULD POOP HERE AGAIN   ★ ★ ★ ★
- ☐ SHIT GOT REAL   ★ ★ ★
- ☐ SAME SHIT DIFFERENT HOUSE   ★ ★
- ☐ THINGS JUST DIDN'T COME OUT RIGHT ★

Welcome! PLEASE SEAT YOURSELF AND ENJOY YOUR VISIT!

NAME: _____ DATE: _____ TIME: _____ DURATION OF VISIT: _____
                                                                                    HRS   MIN   SEC

PURPOSE FOR VISIT: ▢ #1 ▢ #2 ▢ OTHER: _____ SUCCESS? ▢ YES ▢ NO

FAVORITE EUPHEMISM FOR PERFORMING #1:

FAVORITE RESTROOM GRAFFITI OR YOUR ORIGNAL DOODLE:

FAVORITE EUPHEMISM FOR PERFORMING #2:

WHILE YOU WERE HERE, DID YOU:
- ☐ TEXT SOMEONE
- ☐ MAKE A PHONE CALL
- ☐ EMAIL
- ☐ CHECK SOCIAL MEDIA
- ☐ TAKE A SELFIE
- ☐ LOOK IN THE MEDICINE CABINET
- ☐ CHECK YOUR TEETH
- ☐ CHECK OUT YOUR BUTT
- ☐ CHECK YOUR FLY
- ☐ READ
- ☐ FIX YOUR HAIR
- ☐ TAKE SOME EXTRA "ME TIME"
- ☐ TALK TO YOURSELF
- ☐ CONDUCT BUSINESS OTHER THAN YOUR "BUSINESS." CARE TO SHARE?

FAVORITE NAME FOR THIS ROOM:
- ☐ BATHROOM
- ☐ TOILET
- ☐ POWDER ROOM
- ☐ LAVATORY
- ☐ SHITTER
- ☐ LOO
- ☐ LITTLE GIRLS ROOM
- ☐ LITTLE BOYS ROOM
- ☐ COMFORT STATION
- ☐ OTHER: _____
- ☐ JOHN
- ☐ CAN
- ☐ HEAD
- ☐ POTTY
- ☐ CRAPPER
- ☐ WC

RATINGS:
	1	2	3	4	5
CLEANLINESS	☆	☆	☆	☆	☆
AMBIENCE	☆	☆	☆	☆	☆
AMENITIES	☆	☆	☆	☆	☆
SOUND PROOFING	☆	☆	☆	☆	☆
QUALITY OF THE FLUSH	☆	☆	☆	☆	☆
TOILET PAPER	☆	☆	☆	☆	☆

OVERALL EXPERIENCE:
- ☐ BEST SEAT IN THE HOUSE ★ ★ ★ ★ ★
- ☐ WOULD POOP HERE AGAIN ★ ★ ★ ★
- ☐ SHIT GOT REAL ★ ★ ★
- ☐ SAME SHIT DIFFERENT HOUSE ★ ★
- ☐ THINGS JUST DIDN'T COME OUT RIGHT ★

THOUGHTS/MESSAGES: _____
_____
_____

Welcome! PLEASE SEAT YOURSELF AND ENJOY YOUR VISIT!

NAME: _____ DATE: _____ TIME: _____ DURATION OF VISIT: _____

HRS   MIN   SEC

PURPOSE FOR VISIT: 🧻 #1   🧻 #2   🧻 OTHER: _____   SUCCESS? 🧻 YES 🧻 NO

FAVORITE EUPHEMISM FOR PERFORMING #1:

FAVORITE RESTROOM GRAFFITI OR YOUR ORIGNAL DOODLE:

FAVORITE EUPHEMISM FOR PERFORMING #2:

WHILE YOU WERE HERE, DID YOU:

☐ TEXT SOMEONE
☐ MAKE A PHONE CALL
☐ EMAIL
☐ CHECK SOCIAL MEDIA
☐ TAKE A SELFIE
☐ LOOK IN THE MEDICINE CABINET
☐ CHECK YOUR TEETH
☐ CHECK OUT YOUR BUTT
☐ CHECK YOUR FLY
☐ READ
☐ FIX YOUR HAIR
☐ TAKE SOME EXTRA "ME TIME"
☐ TALK TO YOURSELF
☐ CONDUCT BUSINESS OTHER THAN YOUR "BUSINESS." CARE TO SHARE?
_____

FAVORITE NAME FOR THIS ROOM:

☐ BATHROOM
☐ TOILET
☐ POWDER ROOM
☐ LAVATORY
☐ SHITTER
☐ LOO
☐ LITTLE GIRLS ROOM
☐ LITTLE BOYS ROOM
☐ COMFORT STATION
☐ OTHER: _____
☐ JOHN
☐ CAN
☐ HEAD
☐ POTTY
☐ CRAPPER
☐ WC

_____
_____

RATINGS:

	1	2	3	4	5
CLEANLINESS	☆	☆	☆	☆	☆
AMBIENCE	☆	☆	☆	☆	☆
AMENITIES	☆	☆	☆	☆	☆
SOUND PROOFING	☆	☆	☆	☆	☆
QUALITY OF THE FLUSH	☆	☆	☆	☆	☆
TOILET PAPER	☆	☆	☆	☆	☆

OVERALL EXPERIENCE:

☐ BEST SEAT IN THE HOUSE ★★★★★
☐ WOULD POOP HERE AGAIN ★★★★
☐ SHIT GOT REAL ★★★
☐ SAME SHIT DIFFERENT HOUSE ★★
☐ THINGS JUST DIDN'T COME OUT RIGHT ★

THOUGHTS/MESSAGES: _____
_____
_____

Welcome! PLEASE SEAT YOURSELF AND ENJOY YOUR VISIT!

NAME: _____ DATE: _____ TIME: _____ DURATION OF VISIT: _____

HRS   MIN   SEC

PURPOSE FOR VISIT: 🧻 #1   🧻 #2   🧻 OTHER: _____   SUCCESS? 🧻 YES 🧻 NO

FAVORITE EUPHEMISM FOR PERFORMING #1:

FAVORITE RESTROOM GRAFFITI OR YOUR ORIGNAL DOODLE:

FAVORITE EUPHEMISM FOR PERFORMING #2:

WHILE YOU WERE HERE, DID YOU:

- ☐ TEXT SOMEONE
- ☐ MAKE A PHONE CALL
- ☐ EMAIL
- ☐ CHECK SOCIAL MEDIA
- ☐ TAKE A SELFIE
- ☐ LOOK IN THE MEDICINE CABINET
- ☐ CHECK YOUR TEETH
- ☐ CHECK OUT YOUR BUTT
- ☐ CHECK YOUR FLY
- ☐ READ
- ☐ FIX YOUR HAIR
- ☐ TAKE SOME EXTRA "ME TIME"
- ☐ TALK TO YOURSELF
- ☐ CONDUCT BUSINESS OTHER THAN YOUR "BUSINESS." CARE TO SHARE?

FAVORITE NAME FOR THIS ROOM:

- ☐ BATHROOM
- ☐ TOILET
- ☐ POWDER ROOM
- ☐ LAVATORY
- ☐ SHITTER
- ☐ LOO
- ☐ LITTLE GIRLS ROOM
- ☐ LITTLE BOYS ROOM
- ☐ COMFORT STATION
- ☐ OTHER: _____
- ☐ JOHN
- ☐ CAN
- ☐ HEAD
- ☐ POTTY
- ☐ CRAPPER
- ☐ WC

RATINGS:

	1	2	3	4	5
CLEANLINESS	☆	☆	☆	☆	☆
AMBIENCE	☆	☆	☆	☆	☆
AMENITIES	☆	☆	☆	☆	☆
SOUND PROOFING	☆	☆	☆	☆	☆
QUALITY OF THE FLUSH	☆	☆	☆	☆	☆
TOILET PAPER	☆	☆	☆	☆	☆

OVERALL EXPERIENCE:

- ☐ BEST SEAT IN THE HOUSE ★ ★ ★ ★ ★
- ☐ WOULD POOP HERE AGAIN ★ ★ ★ ★
- ☐ SHIT GOT REAL ★ ★ ★
- ☐ SAME SHIT DIFFERENT HOUSE ★ ★
- ☐ THINGS JUST DIDN'T COME OUT RIGHT ★

THOUGHTS/MESSAGES: _____

Welcome! PLEASE SEAT YOURSELF AND ENJOY YOUR VISIT!

NAME: _____ DATE: _____ TIME: _____ DURATION OF VISIT: _____

HRS   MIN   SEC

PURPOSE FOR VISIT: ▢ #1 ▢ #2 ▢ OTHER: _____ SUCCESS? ▢ YES ▢ NO

FAVORITE EUPHEMISM FOR PERFORMING #1:

FAVORITE RESTROOM GRAFFITI OR YOUR ORIGNAL DOODLE:

FAVORITE EUPHEMISM FOR PERFORMING #2:

WHILE YOU WERE HERE, DID YOU:

☐ TEXT SOMEONE
☐ MAKE A PHONE CALL
☐ EMAIL
☐ CHECK SOCIAL MEDIA
☐ TAKE A SELFIE
☐ LOOK IN THE MEDICINE CABINET
☐ CHECK YOUR TEETH
☐ CHECK OUT YOUR BUTT
☐ CHECK YOUR FLY
☐ READ
☐ FIX YOUR HAIR
☐ TAKE SOME EXTRA "ME TIME"
☐ TALK TO YOURSELF
☐ CONDUCT BUSINESS OTHER THAN YOUR "BUSINESS." CARE TO SHARE?
_____

FAVORITE NAME FOR THIS ROOM:

☐ BATHROOM
☐ TOILET
☐ POWDER ROOM
☐ LAVATORY
☐ SHITTER
☐ LOO
☐ LITTLE GIRLS ROOM
☐ LITTLE BOYS ROOM
☐ COMFORT STATION
☐ OTHER: _____
☐ JOHN
☐ CAN
☐ HEAD
☐ POTTY
☐ CRAPPER
☐ WC

_____

RATINGS:	1	2	3	4	5
CLEANLINESS	☆	☆	☆	☆	☆
AMBIENCE	☆	☆	☆	☆	☆
AMENITIES	☆	☆	☆	☆	☆
SOUND PROOFING	☆	☆	☆	☆	☆
QUALITY OF THE FLUSH	☆	☆	☆	☆	☆
TOILET PAPER	☆	☆	☆	☆	☆

OVERALL EXPERIENCE:

☐ BEST SEAT IN THE HOUSE ★ ★ ★ ★ ★
☐ WOULD POOP HERE AGAIN ★ ★ ★ ★
☐ SHIT GOT REAL ★ ★ ★
☐ SAME SHIT DIFFERENT HOUSE ★ ★
☐ THINGS JUST DIDN'T COME OUT RIGHT ★

THOUGHTS/MESSAGES: _____
_____
_____

Welcome! PLEASE SEAT YOURSELF AND ENJOY YOUR VISIT!

NAME: _____ DATE: _____ TIME: _____ DURATION OF VISIT: _____
HRS   MIN   SEC

PURPOSE FOR VISIT: 🧻 #1 🧻 #2 🧻 OTHER: _____ SUCCESS? 🧻 YES 🧻 NO

FAVORITE EUPHEMISM FOR PERFORMING #1:

FAVORITE RESTROOM GRAFFITI OR YOUR ORIGNAL DOODLE:

FAVORITE EUPHEMISM FOR PERFORMING #2:

WHILE YOU WERE HERE, DID YOU:
- ☐ TEXT SOMEONE
- ☐ MAKE A PHONE CALL
- ☐ EMAIL
- ☐ CHECK SOCIAL MEDIA
- ☐ TAKE A SELFIE
- ☐ LOOK IN THE MEDICINE CABINET
- ☐ CHECK YOUR TEETH
- ☐ CHECK OUT YOUR BUTT
- ☐ CHECK YOUR FLY
- ☐ READ
- ☐ FIX YOUR HAIR
- ☐ TAKE SOME EXTRA "ME TIME"
- ☐ TALK TO YOURSELF
- ☐ CONDUCT BUSINESS OTHER THAN YOUR "BUSINESS." CARE TO SHARE?
_____

FAVORITE NAME FOR THIS ROOM:
- ☐ BATHROOM
- ☐ TOILET
- ☐ POWDER ROOM
- ☐ LAVATORY
- ☐ SHITTER
- ☐ LOO
- ☐ LITTLE GIRLS ROOM
- ☐ LITTLE BOYS ROOM
- ☐ COMFORT STATION
- ☐ OTHER: _____
- ☐ JOHN
- ☐ CAN
- ☐ HEAD
- ☐ POTTY
- ☐ CRAPPER
- ☐ WC

RATINGS:
	1 2 3 4 5
CLEANLINESS	☆ ☆ ☆ ☆ ☆
AMBIENCE	☆ ☆ ☆ ☆ ☆
AMENITIES	☆ ☆ ☆ ☆ ☆
SOUND PROOFING	☆ ☆ ☆ ☆ ☆
QUALITY OF THE FLUSH	☆ ☆ ☆ ☆ ☆
TOILET PAPER	☆ ☆ ☆ ☆ ☆

OVERALL EXPERIENCE:
- ☐ BEST SEAT IN THE HOUSE ★ ★ ★ ★ ★
- ☐ WOULD POOP HERE AGAIN ★ ★ ★ ★
- ☐ SHIT GOT REAL ★ ★ ★
- ☐ SAME SHIT DIFFERENT HOUSE ★ ★
- ☐ THINGS JUST DIDN'T COME OUT RIGHT ★

THOUGHTS/MESSAGES: _____
_____
_____

Welcome! PLEASE SEAT YOURSELF AND ENJOY YOUR VISIT!

NAME: _____ DATE: _____ TIME: _____ DURATION OF VISIT: _____

HRS   MIN   SEC

PURPOSE FOR VISIT: [ ] #1 [ ] #2 [ ] OTHER: _____ SUCCESS? [ ] YES [ ] NO

FAVORITE EUPHEMISM FOR PERFORMING #1: | FAVORITE RESTROOM GRAFFITI OR YOUR ORIGNAL DOODLE:

FAVORITE EUPHEMISM FOR PERFORMING #2:

WHILE YOU WERE HERE, DID YOU:
- ☐ TEXT SOMEONE
- ☐ MAKE A PHONE CALL
- ☐ EMAIL
- ☐ CHECK SOCIAL MEDIA
- ☐ TAKE A SELFIE
- ☐ LOOK IN THE MEDICINE CABINET
- ☐ CHECK YOUR TEETH
- ☐ CHECK OUT YOUR BUTT
- ☐ CHECK YOUR FLY
- ☐ READ
- ☐ FIX YOUR HAIR
- ☐ TAKE SOME EXTRA "ME TIME"
- ☐ TALK TO YOURSELF
- ☐ CONDUCT BUSINESS OTHER THAN YOUR "BUSINESS." CARE TO SHARE?
  _____

FAVORITE NAME FOR THIS ROOM:
- ☐ BATHROOM
- ☐ TOILET
- ☐ POWDER ROOM
- ☐ LAVATORY
- ☐ SHITTER
- ☐ LOO
- ☐ LITTLE GIRLS ROOM
- ☐ LITTLE BOYS ROOM
- ☐ COMFORT STATION
- ☐ OTHER: _____

- ☐ JOHN
- ☐ CAN
- ☐ HEAD
- ☐ POTTY
- ☐ CRAPPER
- ☐ WC

THOUGHTS/MESSAGES: _____

RATINGS:

	1	2	3	4	5
CLEANLINESS	☆	☆	☆	☆	☆
AMBIENCE	☆	☆	☆	☆	☆
AMENITIES	☆	☆	☆	☆	☆
SOUND PROOFING	☆	☆	☆	☆	☆
QUALITY OF THE FLUSH	☆	☆	☆	☆	☆
TOILET PAPER	☆	☆	☆	☆	☆

OVERALL EXPERIENCE:
- ☐ BEST SEAT IN THE HOUSE ★ ★ ★ ★ ★
- ☐ WOULD POOP HERE AGAIN ★ ★ ★ ★
- ☐ SHIT GOT REAL ★ ★ ★
- ☐ SAME SHIT DIFFERENT HOUSE ★ ★
- ☐ THINGS JUST DIDN'T COME OUT RIGHT ★

89030504R00057